Finding
Our Way Home

Finding Our Way Home

TURNING BACK TO
WHAT MATTERS MOST

Mark R. McMinn

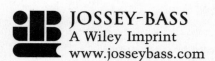

JOSSEY-BASS
A Wiley Imprint
www.josseybass.com

Published by Jossey-Bass
A Wiley Imprint
989 Market Street, San Francisco, CA 94103-1741   www.josseybass.com

Jossey-Bass books and products are available through most bookstores. To contact Jossey-Bass directly call our Customer Care Department within the U.S. at 800-956-7739, outside the U.S. at 317-572-3986 or fax 317-572-4002.

Quote from "As Good as It Gets" granted courtesy of Columbia Tristar Motion Picture Group. Scripture quotations are taken from the Holy Bible, New Living Translation, copyright ©1996. Used by permission of Tyndale House Publishers, Inc., Wheaton, Illinois 60189. All rights reserved.

Jossey-Bass also publishes its books in a variety of electronic formats. Some content that appears in print may not be available in electronic books.

Library of Congress Cataloging-in-Publication Data
McMinn, Mark R.
  Finding our way home: turning back to what matters most/Mark McMinn—1st ed.
      p. cm.
  Includes bibliographical references.
  ISBN 0-7879-7531-1 (alk. paper)
  1. Redemption—Christianity. I. Title.
  BT775.M25 2005
  234'.3—dc22   2004027031

Printed in the United States of America
FIRST EDITION
HB Printing   10 9 8 7 6 5 4 3 2 1

Contents

To Lisa

Acknowledgments

This is a very personal book—one that reflects some of my wanderings through life as well as my journey toward a spiritual home—so my gratitude is also very personal. I am thankful for my family, for their stable love and support. I begin the book by telling a difficult story involving my mother and father, but I have not done justice to their stability and goodness. I love and respect them, and am grateful to share their genes, their culture, and their faith. Lisa McMinn and I have been married for twenty-five years, and I tell stories of her too. Lisa is my colleague, my friend, my lover, and my partner. I am grateful for the touches of grace she brings to my life. And I am grateful that she reads everything I write and helps make it better. My children—Rae, Sarah, and Megan—are grown women now, each of them with unique strengths and talents. They inspire me and help me stay relevant in a changing world.

I tell other people's stories in this book too. I am grateful for every person's story, told and untold, because the stories of life keep us pondering the meaning of it all.

And I feel compelled to thank friends who influenced this book in various ways: sharing personal stories, suggesting books to read, joining me in meaningful conversations and long-term connections that have shaped my understanding of home. Thank you Jeff, Cindy, Clark, Ev, Scott, Amy, Katheryn, Barrett, Ray, Ruth, Zondra, Tracy, and others. We ought to thank friends every chance we get. Even if the thanks are vague and nonspecific, it is so much better to thank our friends and to thank God for our friends than to let them go unnoticed.

Finally, I am grateful for the experts at Jossey-Bass who have helped me craft this book. Sheryl Fullerton, executive editor, has helped and encouraged me every step along the way. She deserves both credit and thanks if there is any good writing to be found among these pages.

February 2005   Mark R. McMinn
                                                   Wheaton, Illinois

Finding
Our Way Home

Introduction

We were eight rebels, eating pasta and garlic bread at the height of the latest low-carbohydrate regime. The Atkins fad of the 1970s resurrected with the new century, bringing new low-carb prophets and more bad news for Wonder Bread. But on this particular February night we were eating retro foods, and none of us seemed troubled by the shifting winds of dietary lore.

We were troubled by the length and depth of another Chicago winter. Like typical Midwesterners, we pined for the rebounding temperatures of spring before whining that spring lasts only a few days in Chicago, those magical moments squeezed into the fourth week of the Cubs season, between the last April snowstorm and the sweltering heat of summer. Everyone who has been to Wrigley Field knows it is a microcosm of the Midwest—always too cold or too hot. In Colorado it is sunny three hundred days a year. In Chicago we complain three hundred days a year. It's a cultural thing. We complain and ask someone to please pass the pasta.

A huge print of Rembrandt's painting *The Return of the Prodigal Son* was hanging in our hosts' townhouse dining room. I had just finished writing a book that used the same painting as a metaphor for sin and grace, and had even traveled to St. Petersburg, Russia, to see Rembrandt's original in the State Hermitage Museum. *Why Sin Matters* had not yet been released, and because I have less than an ounce of salesmanship and only about a pound of extraversion lurking in my 170-pound frame, few at the dinner party knew I had written it or had any special connection with the painting. If others had known, perhaps they would have understood my distraction throughout the conversation. My eyes and my attention kept wandering back to the painting. I was happy with the book I had just finished, but I knew there was something unfinished in those soon-to-be-published pages. The story of our lives, and the story of Rembrandt's painting, is one of sin and grace, but it is also one of losing and redis-covering the safety and security of home.

Rembrandt's painting is loosely based on a story Jesus told about a foolish young son who despised the constraints of home. He tired of waiting for his father to die, so he asked for his share of the inheritance early and then traveled to a far-away land, where he squandered it on wild living. When the money ran out, the destitute young man had no way to make a living. He took a job feeding pigs, where he was so fam-ished—with a hunger that was not simply physical—that he longed to eat the slop he was feeding the swine. And then he remembered a father who loved him, and he began yearning for the security of home.

Have you, like the Prodigal Son, ever stood in a place wondering what to do next, how to recover from a terrible decision or a devastating set of events? If you have, I suspect you recognize a deep, primordial hunger for home that is more poignant than a growling stomach or shrinking waistline.

The home the Prodigal Son longed for—and the one we all seek—is a place of secure love, known most fully in the embrace of God. The great mystery and paradox of home is found in its familiarity and unfamiliarity. We are familiar with home because of occasional sightings. Sometimes we glimpse home in ourselves, in the deepest movements of our souls, as we set aside the distractions and insecurities of daily life and sit calmly in the presence of the divine. We see home in some relationships, when compassion and trust and honesty converge into places of deep safety and comfort that surely reflect God's goodness. We get occasional glimpses of home in our communities, when we rise up beyond our normal self-protective impulses and begin to listen to and care for one another in ways that transform and heal and call us to deeper experiences of faith and faithfulness. In the midst of such security a person garners the courage to face new challenges, to venture out and explore the world.

Yet home is simultaneously unfamiliar, never quite fulfilled. As a result, much of life's venturing out is secretly motivated by our lifelong quest for Eden. Urges for secure love keep us searching, but we encounter so much disappointment. The ecstasy of deep prayer is shattered by the blare of the cell phone or the distraction of today's busy schedule. Close relationships are tainted with misunderstandings, demands, selfish ambition, and unfaithful hearts. Communities may have moments of greatness, but those moments are scattered sporadically through long stretches of unremarkable routine. We have seen enough of home to keep us questing for more, but hardly enough to believe we have truly experienced it.

Each time I see Rembrandt's painting, I am reminded that the oscillations of life are not limited to nutritional crazes or the temperature at Wrigley Field or even the tendency for my attention to wander. Throughout each of our lives we move in and out of loving embraces, meandering off to faraway lands, both because the measure of secure love we have known allows us to venture outward and because we always seem to be searching for more. Ultimately we wake up to the truth that our explorations have taken us nowhere near paradise. We so easily wander from the relationships, values, and beliefs we cherish, often searching for the very things we are leaving behind.

"Mark, can you pass me the salad dressing?" I started as I realized I had been lost in contemplation of the painting when I was interrupted by Ryan, the young man sitting to my right.

"Sure. Here you go. Isn't it an amazing print?" Convicted by my lack of attentiveness, I thought Ryan might prefer to join me in my reverie rather than continue in silence. Our conversation lingered over Rembrandt's genius before turning to Ryan's recent outing to Mel Gibson's movie *The Passion of the Christ.* Our discussion turned from one art form to another while remaining on the same topic.

"Do you know what I felt as I left that movie?" Ryan queried. "I felt so convicted about my sin that I never wanted to sin again. Of course now a couple weeks have passed, and I realize I can never overcome my sin altogether." I remembered Augustine's phrase *non posse non peccare,* it is not possible for us not to sin. Gibson, Rembrandt, Augustine, Ryan, and I were all saying the same thing: we wander off despite deep conviction and noble effort. Sometimes we set aside our values and wander off in search of wanton excitement, as the Prodigal did. Of course wandering is not only about sin. It is about our quest to find something more, some rest and safety and comfort, but we so easily get lost.

Jesus offers hope. The story he told of the Prodigal Son does not end at a pigsty in a faraway land. In a profound turn toward redemption, the Prodigal "came to his senses," realizing that he could return and ask his father to let him work as a servant. At least then, he reasoned, he would have food to eat. So he trudged back along the road that once led him away from everything he knew, practicing a speech of repentance with the hope that his father might take him back in a much humbler role. But his father, who must have made a habit of looking down the road, saw him coming from a distance and ran to greet him. As the son delivered his rehearsed speech, the father embraced the Prodigal and welcomed him home—not as a servant but as a long-lost son. Then they had a party, complete with dancing and laughter and plenty of roast beef.

This is the moment Rembrandt (and so many others) captured in his painting, an image that has shaped art and literature and all sorts of human experience over the past two millennia. On Rembrandt's canvas, as in so many artistic portrayals of the Prodigal Son, we see our common human yearning to know, to find, and to inhabit that *place of secure love, known most fully in the embrace of God.*

TURNS TOWARD REDEMPTION

This book calls us to yearn together, to risk reaching out, to grow deep as we explore the pains and joys of the past, contemplate the profound beauty that awaits us, ponder the restlessness that besets us, and name the many ways we disguise our true longings for home. It is divided into four parts. The first, "Contours of Home," explores further this notion of a turn toward redemption.

Human life transpires at the intersection of two paradoxical forces. One force draws us toward *shalom*—a deep abiding place of safety and repose (*shalom* is a Hebrew word that is a traditional Jewish greeting). The second force sends us outward toward adventure and exploration. These two forces are not necessarily in opposition, but often we live as if they are, wandering like prodigals far from shalom in our search for conquest and discovery. But God created us to hunger for shalom, to turn around, redirect our steps, and find our way home. There is a redemptive rhythm here. To redeem means to buy back, and God specializes in bringing wanderers back, guiding us home to a place of shalom.

As the Prodigal Son and his father embrace, so the reality of our pain clings to the promise of love fulfilled in the life of faith. All the oscillations of life are once again rooted in the hope that God is bigger than our capricious whims, our existential loneliness, and our deepest rebellion.

As you have probably detected, I write this book as a Christian, which means that I cling to a particular metanarrative about home. This grand story begins with the assumption that humans were designed for some beautiful place of wholeness where we walk and talk with one another and with God in perfect shalom. But this is also a story of crisis. Gibson told Jay Leno that the Bible should be R-rated (in response to complaints about the violence in *The Passion of the Christ*). Perhaps he is right. Creation was and is ruptured by rebellion, and as a result we wander through life searching for that home that we only faintly recall. It's nasty out here—full of dangers and snares. The good news is that the Christian story is a story of homecoming, one in which Eden is reclaimed and shalom restored. Homecoming does not just involve heaven, our ultimate hope, but also the glimpses of redemption we see around us every day.

Even if you do not share my Christian assumptions, perhaps you feel a pull toward, a yearning for a secure love that reverberates through all time and all creation. Instinctively we know that we are made to enjoy something beautiful and good, yet we too easily and too often settle for something less.

The notion of a turn toward redemption is built on three assumptions, each of which we will pursue in the first part of this book. First, coming home implies that we once lived in a place of joy and goodness, or at least that we have longed for such a place. Your childhood home may have been a place of safety and love, or it may have been more like the Prodigal's life at the pig farm. Most likely it was some (or sum) of both. But even if your childhood home was an utter mess, or if your home today is a mess, you probably long for something better. And that longing validates your inkling (and mine) that we are created to cherish shalom. Chapter One explores our intuitive inclination toward home.

Second, a turn toward redemption implies that we have drifted off, or perhaps darted off, from the shalom found in God's love. Life fluctuates, and so do we. We face distraction and struggle and self-deceit, and we are drawn to the grand adventures of the future. Life wounds us and woos us. Not surprisingly, we head out looking for a better way. The wandering itself is not a problem. Indeed, it reflects aliveness and energy and a sort of holy disappointment that keeps us searching for the noblest parts of human existence. But we easily wander too far or leave too soon or head off in the wrong directions. The human quest for meaning easily devolves into selfish pursuit of pleasure, and because our human calculus for minimizing pain and maximizing pleasure is badly skewed, we end up finding varieties of pleasure that evaporate long before they fulfill any of our deepest needs. Chapter Two reminds us that we are like hitchhikers, venturing out in search of something important but looking for something deeper than we know.

Third, a turn toward redemption suggests that we eventually come to our senses, turn around, and reclaim something that was lost. We all want to find our way back to places of safety and security, where the dangers of the world occur on the other side of a white picket fence. Home is simply a metaphor, of course, but a powerful one. We search for places of predictability, where routines remind us that dinner is at six and that there is order in the cosmos. In our hope for such a home, there is to be celebration, with laughter filling the family room and memories lining the hallways in picture frames of various shapes and sizes. We picture home as a place of beauty, where it is worth our time to mop the floors and paint the trim, and where we find loveliness in the faces of those we love. Home is where relationships last a lifetime, even surviving the vicissitudes of rebellion and trauma. Home as a metaphor is all these things—safety, predictability, celebration, beauty, and relationship—but real life is probably nowhere close to the metaphor. Our days are tainted with misunderstanding and selfishness, with wandering hearts and painful glances, with disappointment and disillusionment, with fear and anger and sadness and grief, and sometimes with abandonment and abuse. But it is precisely in the midst of real life that we glimpse a deep yearning inside to turn toward redemption. We turn, literally and metaphorically, toward a home that holds the promise of shalom we have always yearned to know. And in the turning we begin to see beyond the brokenness of our world to glimpse the bigger truths that tug at our souls.

In this journey home we begin to see things differently. Seeing beyond our weakness, we reclaim our identity as noble children of a good Creator. We discern beauty in the eyes of another and receive comfort in the quiet words of a loved one. Worship begins to resonate with some deep inner cadence of the soul that is easily muffled by life's distractions, and with renewed worship we again hear quiet whispers of God's presence and feel fresh breezes of grace. We recover the right to serve and cherish those we choose to love, because there is almost always something worth celebrating and redeeming in even the most challenging relationships. Chapter Three is an invitation, perhaps even a challenge, to turn and begin reclaiming what we have lost.

LOOKING BACK, LOOKING AROUND, LOOKING UP

The second part of the book is "Looking Back." Chapter Four presents a choice we have to make: we can charge forward in life without stopping to reflect on the past, or we can deliberately look back to remember and grieve and rejoice and wonder. Finding our way home requires courage because it involves turning around, looking back, contemplating both the pain and the joy, and making connections between past and present. It is not easy to look back, because everyone's past is a complex mixture of goodness and brokenness, but choosing to remember ultimately leads to greater peace and health than trying to disregard the past.

Looking back is also a spiritual task, calling us to remember God in all of life. But as important as it is to remember God, this is a backward notion. We can only remember God because God remembered us first. Chapter Five provides a glimpse of the incarnation and its implications for the way we live in faith. Because of the incarnation, we can rest assured that God deems us important, knows us intimately, and loves us dearly.

One of the great challenges of looking back is facing our need to forgive and be forgiven. It is also one of the great blessings. Chapter Six suggests that the ideal context for forgiveness occurs at the intersection of remembering our past and resting in the truth that God remembers us.

The third part of the book is "Looking Around." Superimposed on the story of the past is a longing to find a home in the present. We do not only look back; we also look around. Chapter Seven is an invitation to discover our true self in God. It is so easy to construct false selves, to form our identity around accomplishments or possessions, to assume the road to happiness is paved with selfish ambition. The call toward home is the call to discover the true self that God created each of us to be.

We also find our way home to relationships. Each of us is made for relationship, and it is here we find our greatest contentment in life, but we must also admit that relationships can be difficult, even excruciating at times. Chapter Eight is about finding our way back to those we love, and looking for a deeper healing in those times when relationships are so broken that they cannot be recovered.

The final part of the book is "Looking Up." I mean this in two ways. First, as we'll see in Chapter Nine, we look up in the midst of messy lives to find God. God is revealed in Jesus, full of truth and grace. There is no greater quest in life and death than finding our way home to Jesus.

Looking up also has a future dimension, which is explored in Chapter Ten. Looking up toward heaven—our glorious eternal home—has given hope to people of faith throughout the centuries. Heaven's light is so bright that it illumines memories of the past, shines on today's path, and warms us with the promise of the future. Christians believe that however tattered, lonely, and tired we may be at the end of this life, there is one awaiting who will see us from a distance and run to greet us, embrace us with an eternal love that has no measure, forgive our many sins, and welcome us home to that place we have always belonged but have never seen.

I cannot recall what great physical damage carbohydrates are alleged to do, but we survived their effects that cold February night. We all managed to rise from our chairs and put on our winter coats. The conversation had waned, and the toddlers in the other room were melting down. One by one or two by two, we tugged ourselves away from our friends' warm town-house into the frigid night to warm up our cars. The temperature was brutal—the kind that makes nostril hairs freeze. We complained once more and wished for spring. Then we all headed home.

PART ONE

Contours
of Home

1

The Pull Toward Home

My daughter wanted to hitchhike from Montana to Michigan and back again, so I did what middle-aged fathers do best: I woke at 2 A.M. worrying about it. Rae was almost twenty-three at the time, so there wasn't much I could do to stop her. This delightful young woman—who brings a contented smile to my face when I think of her—is brimming with adventure and independence. When she called with her hitchhiking plan, I protested for a time and then pronounced that if she lives to be thirty she will probably have a wonderful life. Perhaps by then, I thought, she will have enough wisdom to balance her daring spirit. Several years ago my wife, Lisa, wrote a book called *Growing Strong Daughters*. It worked. We grew three Very Strong Daughters. Now I tell her she should write a sequel, *Coping with Strong Daughters*.

Perhaps I am a light sleeper, or maybe it is just that 2 A.M. is ideally suited for the contemplative in me. Many years ago I gave up fretting about being too sleep-deprived to function the next day, and now I mostly enjoy unexpected middle-of-the-night awakenings as opportunities to mull over the contours of home. Sometimes I resort to worry—as I did the night after Rae's hitchhiking pronouncement—but most often it is a time of grateful reflection, prayer, imagination, and anticipation. Sometimes I gaze at Lisa as she sleeps, thanking God for blessing me with such a partner, and wonder where the years have gone. Sometimes I count other blessings. There are many more blessings than sheep in the world, and blessings are easier to count because they do not all look the same. Sometimes I pray for those I love—my family and friends—and for those whom I am still learning to love. Sometimes I think back, remembering earlier days of life, reliving poignant moments, regretting the selfish grasp of sin that I know too well, and basking in the amazement of God's grace that is so much bigger than my sin. Sometimes I think about the accelerating pace of life and wonder what it will be like eventually to pass through the fearful gate of death. I picture what waits on the other side. Though I fight against doubts that linger uninvited in the agnostic shadows of my faith, most often I dare to dream of a place of utter peace and goodness. And sometimes, as I imagine that place of exquisite beauty where I am embraced by a God who loves boundlessly, I slip back into a peaceful sleep until a playful bird outside or a golden oldie from the clock radio wakes me for a new day.

I am not alone. Most of us—perhaps all of us—spend ample time mulling over the stories of our lives. What wakes you in the early morning hours, easing into the quiet of your consciousness? What keeps your mind occupied late at night as the repose of sleep eludes you? Maybe you choose better times than the middle of the night for these quiet moments of reflection, and find your mind wandering as you are sitting in traffic, waiting in the grocery line, sitting in a meeting, sipping a mocha, or walking in the park.

As we reflect and ponder, a common task motivates our thoughts. Each of us is building a story—a pathway to explain where we have been and where we are going. We are making sense of things, looking at the past in the light of the present and the present in the light of the past, forecasting a future and, perhaps, daring to place our fragile hopes in it. We are placing ourselves in context, both historically and interpersonally, as we think about friends and lovers, hitchhiking daughters and risk-taking sons, communities to which we belong, themes of the past and dreams for the future. We tell ourselves the stories of our lives even as we are living them out.

If you and I live for seventy-five years, and if we spend five hours of each week contemplating the story of our lives (it is probably far more), then we will devote over a million minutes to the task over the course of our lifetime. And if our dreams at night are also spent figuring out the meaning of life, then we should double or triple this number. We are people with stories, and our stories reverberate in our minds, relationships, dreams, wishes, and goals.

LEANING TOWARD HOME

Although each of our stories is different, I am writing this book because I believe a common theme runs through them. In one way or another, our stories are about finding pathways toward home. There is a homeward lilt in our step, an inclination of our hearts toward that which is familiar and safe. When I say we lean toward home, I mean it on multiple levels.

At one level it is very literal. We want to be home when we are stuck in traffic. We want those we love to be home—physically and emotionally—so that we can share our lives together. As Rae contemplated her hitchhiking adventure, I wanted her to make it home, to get back safely to her rented house in Missoula where she could resume her normal life: reading at coffee shops, biking and backpacking in the mountains, hanging out with friends, and working at the Americorp position that keeps her a hair's width above the poverty line.

When I travel, especially when I travel overseas, I am eager to come home to Illinois as the trip nears completion. There is something deeply comforting about being home and something transient and disquieting about being away. Those stationed at faraway military bases eagerly await the day when their tours are complete, as loved ones place magnetic calendars on the refrigerator and tally the days until the anticipated homecoming.

Home calls to us, tugs at our emotions, pulls us back to places of familiarity. Even those who have rarely had a home—such as foster children—yearn for its imagined refuge and respite. It is such a strong idea, such a powerful metaphor, that we yearn for it even when we have not had a happy or real experience of its power.

At some deeper level most of us feel the tug of home in a figurative sense. Some worry because a teenage child who resides two doors down the hallway seems to live far from home in every meaningful way. Sometimes we lie awake thinking how far away from home we ourselves have drifted.

What started as a small temptation has become a runaway train—a major life crisis. Or perhaps you are in a marriage that seems far from home—two souls sharing a bed and nothing else. For some it is the unresolved challenges of a childhood home that keep bubbling up and making a mess of life.

At still another level we yearn for an ultimate, even transcendent, home. Sometimes we see through the fog of our daily distractions and recognize how much we yearn for God, for our spiritual home, for that divine embrace of spiritual centeredness that tells us all will be well even when life seems difficult. Maybe you, like me, find yourself longing more for your heavenly home with the passing years, because many of those years expose new layers of loss and brokenness. We find ourselves marching slower with the tempo of aging, facing the fact that some of our hopes and dreams may not be realized this side of eternity. Often we are disappointed and disillusioned with the unfolding drama of life. But even our capacity for disappointment speaks to some intrinsic knowledge that things should be better.

Longing for home is good, a winsome reflection of the way we are created. God is tugging at our hearts, inviting us back to the security of divine love. Intuitively, we know we are crafted by God for something beautiful, and we yearn for it, but this longing is simultaneously sad, reminding us that life in this world is not always as tidy as we wish. Spiritual writers have often referred to life as a pilgrimage, a journey in which we mature through toil and struggle, all the time yearning for another day. This is the great paradox of yearning: it reveals both our noblest desires and our greatest burdens.

PHONING HOME

Some days we glimpse our yearnings more clearly than others. I recall a day in 1993 when I was far from home—more than two thousand miles away from my family in Illinois. I spent the first part of the day taking an intense six-hour oral exam for board certification in my discipline. Within the first twenty minutes I knew that the examining committee was not about to pass me. I found the next five hours and forty minutes agonizing, shaming, and brutally demoralizing. And that was the easy part of my day.

The next part involved driving an hour to my parents' house—the house where I grew up—to discuss their recent decision to be divorced after nearly forty years of marriage. My sister and I both knew it was the only decision that made sense in their situation, but nevertheless our family discussion that evening, and the subsequent losses, would be excruciating. The shame I felt earlier in the day, failing an exam I had spent two years preparing for, was trivial compared to the shame my parents—both of them good parents—felt in ending their marriage. I had my own sadness to bear with the dissolution of my family of origin, but it was even more difficult to watch their pain. It still is.

Between those two events, as I drove down the Sunset Highway west of Portland, I had a compelling urge—like ET in Stephen Spielberg's 1982 movie—to phone home. At the next exit I found a pay phone, called home to Lisa's familiar and comforting voice, and my soul burst. Without even offering perfunctory small talk I began weeping uncontrollably. These were not the tender tears of a sensitive man, but a child's heaving sobs erupting in a grown man's body, as if something I had held back for many years could no longer be contained. I cannot recall another time since childhood when crying had such power over me. Between breathing spasms I spoke of my dismal performance on the exam and how I dreaded the evening ahead. Lisa did what I hoped she would do: she sutured my ruptured soul with her listening ear, her kind words of empathy, and her expressions of love. After twenty minutes of comfort I wiped the tears from my cheeks, climbed back into my rental car, and continued down the Sunset Highway.

At that point in my life, in 1993, Lisa and I had recently come through some difficult years. I wasn't sure how she would respond to my vulnerable cry for help. Yet still I yearned to call, because intuitively I knew that my partner of many years was as close to an earthly home as I could find. Her soft words seeped deep into my being, comforted me, and reminded me how much I need her. Lisa and I both recall that broken day as a profound moment of connection and renewal in our marriage. It was a moment of coming home to a place of secure love. Those twenty minutes of conversation, punctuated by pay-phone static, brought together the paradox of life.

Everything good and everything broken converged in those moments of talking with Lisa. We live in a toilsome and broken world, constantly surrounded by struggle, yet we are also immersed in the hope of love. On that day I felt as though my professional life was a failure, but that was just the surface story. When my emotions erupted, I knew there was a deeper story that could never fit into a primitive taxonomy of good and bad because that story—like all of our lives—was a convoluted mixture of both.

THREE DIMENSIONS OF HOME

Longing for home has three dimensions: past, present, and future. We look back to the past, remembering the good, regretting the bad, wondering how things could have been different with some different choices. As we look back to memories of days gone by, we also look around to contemplate life in our present-day existence. Whether you live alone in a basement apartment or are part of a bustling multigenerational family in a three-story farmhouse, you are probably trying to make sense of it all—to connect the joys and sorrows of yesterday with the opportunities and challenges of today. And of course, we look ahead to the future—wondering, planning, dreaming, fearing.

Past

I have had more than a decade to reflect on that phone call to Lisa and the deep primordial emotion that erupted that afternoon, and I now recognize what I saw only dimly then: the deepest currents of pain were about a grown man looking back, wishing to cling to the security of childhood. I wanted to put on my baseball glove and play catch with my dad in the front yard or to walk in the back door of our farmhouse and be carried away by the aroma of my mother's latest homemade pie. Maybe we could climb in the old Chevy and drive north to the Puget Sound for a vacation like we used to do. Perhaps the Coleman camp stove would still be in the cellar, and once again I could wake from a good night's sleep in the big green and yellow tent to the smell of bacon and the promise of a good day together as a family. All the good memories, all the beautiful things of childhood, were swirling in my mind, and I longed to have them back. My family of origin—which, like most families, had always been a mix of beautiful and broken things—was about to become visibly shattered. I knew it had to be this way, but I wished it didn't. I looked back and longed for the security of long ago.

As I have talked with hundreds of others about their childhoods, I have discovered that my journey is not unique. We look back with wistfulness, sorrow, celebration, remorse, and all sorts of other emotions.

Your life and mine are real and immediate, but they also reflect the greater story of the cosmos. We are a story within a story. Humans were created in the Garden, in a perfect home, teeming with life, filled with wondrous sounds, glorious colors, and fragrant smells. In Eden there was harmony, laughter, connection with God, and safe intimacy between Adam and Eve. In the beginning God created a place of secure love.

We no longer live in Eden, yet we are close enough to catch a glimpse every now and then. And with each glimpse we yearn to be back in a place of perfect peace and acceptance. I agree with psychologist and spiritual director David Benner, who said, "Deep down . . . something within us seems to remember the Garden within which we once existed. Part of us longs to return; we know that this is where we belong."[1]

Weeping in that phone booth along the Sunset Highway was all about that longing to return. With my tears I cried out to be back in the Garden of my childhood, playing catch with my dad, enjoying a long conversation with my mom, or laughing with her because she made six varieties of blueberry pie to see which one the family liked best, singing happy songs about another good day. We were created for Eden, but we live east of Eden.

Present

Living here in the present means living in paradox. We envision neat and tidy homes, with attractive gables, weather-resistant vinyl siding, and shiny new plumbing, but so often we end up mopping flooded basements, letting every possible horizontal surface accumulate with junk mail and other clutter, and living life to the endless rhythm of a dripping faucet. Our homes, like our lives, are complex. We long for peace and repose as we walk in the door, and sometimes we find it. Other times we enter into conflict, cynicism, bitterness, and the scars of unhealed wounds. For some, home is a place of comfort and sanctuary from the tumults of life, at least some of the time. For others, it is a place to yearn for such things. And in the yearning we again see our instinctual leaning toward places of secure love. Even those who have never known a good home know enough to be depressed about it, or angry, or dissatisfied with life. They know they are created for something better than they have experienced.

On that dismal day in 1993 I missed Lisa—not just because I had been out of town for a few days, but because Lisa and I have crafted a lump of familiarity together that we know as our home. Like our tangible home, our relational home is not perfect—we have some leaky faucets in our marriage—but it is a place of refuge and encouragement and hope. Close relationships are like that. Each of us has relational homes with friends, family members, communities of faith, or lifelong partners.

Again, the story functions on two levels—the immediate and the metaphorical. The here and now is real enough: the leaky faucets and vinyl siding, the laughter filling the family room, the lint filter on the clothes dryer that we forget to clean, the gentle words of understanding, the stacks of junk mail, the children who pretend to cringe as their old parents kiss, the hassles over who sweeps the floor or sanitizes the toilet, the embraces of love. But there is another story, a grand story, and it has a here and now also. That is the story that began with Eden and ends with heaven, and it sometimes seems that forever got sandwiched in between. It is a story of a God who invites us into relationship.

It is sometimes difficult to see that God loves us more than we can imagine, and always has, and continually calls us to rest in a place of secure love. Most of us look for love elsewhere, thinking it will be more tangible or powerful or immediate than God's love. We easily wander down the path that leads away from God, squandering our inheritance on that which we hope will bring pleasure, even as over and over we find it brings no joy. Yet we are not forgotten. Gazing down the long, dusty road that once carried us far away, God eagerly awaits our return. Our divine Father is poised to run and embrace each of us—though we are befuddled and wayward prodigals—and throw a homecoming party in our honor. Sometimes in the still of the night, or in the majestic beauty of a snow-capped mountain, we can hear the thunderous rhythm of God running to meet us, to welcome us home.

Someday the security of God's love will be very tangible, but for now it is fuzzy and indistinct in our vision. Sometimes we experience it indirectly through the beauty of prairie grass, the gracious smile of a forgiving companion, a body that heals from infections and diseases, laughter in the company of good friends, and the simple goodness of life's many blessings.

Some have grown deep enough in faith to see God's love in their struggles and pains, perhaps even in the face of death. They have grown deep through the discipline of prayer. When we pray, we catch glimpses of the one who invented love. Spiritual writer Richard Foster states it so winsomely: "And he is inviting you—and me—to come home, to come home to where we belong, to come home to that for which we were created. His arms are stretched out wide to receive us. . . . For too long we have been in a far country; a country of noise and hurry and crowds, a country of climb and push and shove, a country of frustration and fear and intimidation. And he welcomes us home: home to serenity and peace and joy, home to friendship and fellowship and openness, home to intimacy and acceptance and affirmation."[2]

Foster is not referring to shopping-list prayer: "God, give me this and a little of that, and please hurry up because I've already been waiting a long time." Instead, he refers to prayer that aligns our hearts with the pulse of God's presence in the cosmos. In this sort of prayer we learn to listen, to sit in awareness of God's presence, to love the things God loves and to hate the things God hates. Foster refers to prayer as a way of life, a posture of humility in the presence of the divine. It is this sort of prayer that leads us home to God as we learn to rest in the safety of divine love.

Future

Home also has a future tense. Though I didn't recognize it at the time, my angst at that pay phone and my desire for home were also directed forward. Without even knowing it I was looking ahead, drawing on my Christian faith to understand the present in light of the future. Several weeks later my eleven-year-old daughter, Sarah, asked if her grandparents would be married in heaven. Her question took me by surprise. As I stumbled through a sophomoric answer, I began anticipating a place where sadness is consumed by joy. It is hard to picture our new creation—the new heaven and new earth—but I suspect there will be green and yellow tents and baseball mitts and countless opportunities for healing conversations. I imagine the homecoming feast described in the Bible will include families and stepfamilies spanning dozens of generations. The wounds of the past will be set aside, and we will celebrate a new home where everything is set right.

My musings in response to Sarah's question were founded on my Christian faith, which at this point in the middle of my life shapes the way I see everything. I believe we are people with a future that will last much longer than our present bodies. If you are like me, you are skilled at ignoring this—going about daily business as if the matters of this mortal life deserve your full attention. Many of us work, raise children, get promoted, coach Little League, save for retirement, buy a house, travel, retire on a lake in the Ozarks, and life goes on. Or does it? Eventually it ends. Beneath each life event there is a subtle motif of immortality, the possibility of heaven, which always lurks in the background. This is our telos instinct—the hope of an ultimate Home that draws us beyond the details of daily life to look for a loving God. If home is a place of secure love, it is most surely found in the arms of the one who loves us first.

Pastor and author Mark Buchanan writes of our instinctual longing for heaven in his book *Unseen Things*. He was asked to preach at a funeral service, and after almost two hours of testimonials from friends of the deceased he tossed aside the notes he had prepared and simply spoke of the possibility of Home:

> I don't care what religion you belong to or would never belong to, what beliefs you profess or scorn. I would bet a sweet purse that every one of you in this room has an instinct, and that the instinct is sharp as a razor right now. The instinct is that the world is not enough. The instinct is that this world isn't big enough, long enough, deep enough to contain or explain even one single life in it. The instinct is that death, no matter how natural its causes, is always unnatural, a brusque intruder, a gloating enemy, and that death shouldn't be allowed to have the last word. The instinct is that we weren't made for this world only. We were made for eternity. The world is not enough. Did you think it was?[3]

The Christian story ends in a place of perfect peace. We believe our sins are already forgiven, but in heaven they will be removed. And we will no longer be held hostage by the sins of others. There will be no more survivors of sexual abuse, no more gambling addictions, no selfish spouses, no hunger or racism or oppression of any form. Everything will be right again, and we will be back home as if we never left—still nestled in the Garden, basking in the radiant light of God's glory and breathing in the comfort of eternal love.

THE SOJOURNERS' WAY

So it is. We sojourn as children of Adam and Eve in a broken world, instinctually longing for that place of life and comfort and rest that we call home. Although these yearnings are somewhat bound to the here and now—where we have pay phones and divorce—they also reflect something more eternal and foundational. We long for a place of rest and security that can never fully be found in our earthly pilgrimage. Whether we look back toward Eden or forward toward heaven, it is the same inner urge that compels us to reach beyond the nomadic existence of this broken world and to search for our true spiritual home. As spiritual writer Frederick Buechner reminds us, we are not living in "the last truth about the world but only the next to the last truth."[4]

When we look around the nooks and crannies of our lives, we see this yearning for the last truth—for home—everywhere. Even if we fail to recognize home's pull, we cannot escape its influence. From the moment our eyes crack open in the early morning until our weary bodies fall into bed at night, we are filled with a desire for home. And in the in-between times, as we drift into our dreams, our hearts and minds are still pulling us home.

2

A Hitchhiker's Guide

My daughter Rae decided not to hitchhike. She and a friend drove her aging Ford Ranger instead and made it safely home. Life is good.

I have never tried hitchhiking, have never been attracted to the idea, and certainly have never pictured my daughter thumbing her way down the highway until that ominous pronouncement that left me worrying in the wee hours of the morning. The closest I have come to hitchhiking is to read Douglas Adams's book *The Hitchhiker's Guide to the Galaxy*, and even that wasn't much about hitchhiking. After reading the book twice and being enormously entertained both times, I'm still not sure what that book is about. But it's not about hitchhiking.

Still, hitchhiking—in all its splendor and horror—is an effective metaphor for life's journey. If the teeter-totter of life has adventure on one end and security on the other, then we can learn from the hitchhiker's spontaneous ways while remembering that security provides the counterbalance every rambler needs. We venture out to explore the world, to know the thrill of new discovery. In the process we grow, learn, and conquer many fears, all the while remembering places of familiar security and safety.

I can think of at least five ways that hitchhiking is like life.

LIFE IS AN UNPREDICTABLE ADVENTURE

Hitchhikers move from Point A to Point B without the security of firm plans. I suspect this is part of the thrill of hitchhiking—enjoying the wind-in-your-hair freedom and the open adventure of the road. Hitchhikers have no delusions of planning their travel in advance, so they remain open to possibilities and savor the unpredictability of their journey. And when the adventure is over they typically come home, from Point B to Point A. We are always moving in relation to home; we can always see home through the front windshield or in the rearview mirror.

There is a rhythm here: venturing out in an unpredictable and unsafe world, then coming home to safety. Both are important. We breathe out, we breathe in. We move away, we come back home. Mark Buchanan describes it as two simultaneous impulses, the first to go beyond, to adventure outward, to be footloose, the second to come home, to find safety and comfort: "to dig back down to the bedrock, curl back into the womb. We cherish the familiar. We long for the way we were. We seek safety, domesticity, serenity—to find again that which we've lost."[1] The repose of coming home is found on the other side of our drive for adventure.

Hitchhikers seem to understand something about embracing adventure, even if it seems a bit over the edge of wisdom for many of us. To illustrate this point, consider two imaginary travelers. One should have a name that reminds us of spontaneity and freedom, or at least of trail mix and backpacks. Something like Cypress or Braxton or Marigold would do well. If we succumb to stereotypic license we might speculate that this person eats tofu pizza, carries a ceramic mug from one espresso shop to the next in order to save the trees used to make paper cups, and uses toothpaste that tastes as bad as the pine needles from which it must have been derived. The other name should be predictable and settled—something like James or Deborah or Michael. This person drives a Buick, buys Nikes instead of Tevas, and watches the evening news.

So let's say that Braxton is heading out on a hitchhiking trip across the country; Michael is planning to drive the same basic distance. Michael gets the oil changed in his car before leaving, packs a cooler with soft drinks that have first resided a few hours in the freezer, takes money for restaurant stops, and makes reservations at motels with swimming pools along the freeway. His trip from Point A to Point B is complete with the comfort of firm mattresses, hot meals, and familiar beverages. Meanwhile Braxton sits alongside the freeway or in the backseat of a stranger's smoke-filled sedan, without knowing where the next meal or the next night's sleep will be. Braxton's life is more chaotic and dangerous, but in some strange way Braxton is free. He has no pressure to make it to Denver by Thursday or to the Holiday Inn in Kansas City before 6 P.M. Braxton stops to picnic by a lake in Arkansas; Michael barrels down the freeway to stay on schedule.

Which is more like life: Braxton's spontaneous adventure or Michael's triple-A travel planning approach? The answer, of course, is that healthy living brings Braxton and Michael together. Those who cannot find balance on this teeter-totter of adventure and safety face various troubles. The thrill seeker who can never settle down ends up living a short life, often marked with restlessness, broken relationships, and discontent—or even worse. The tidy curmudgeon who never deviates from the predictable ends up idolizing security until the security turns and attacks itself, he loses the control he so loves, and fear takes over.

When we try to insulate ourselves with a predictable life, our plans invariably fail. Life is not predictable. We cannot know what will happen later today or tomorrow, and if we fail to see life as adventure, then we are destined to disappointment. Michael's soft drink container expands too much in the freezer and makes a sticky mess of the cooler as it thaws. The motel swimming pool is closed for repairs. The car breaks down on the Missouri Interstate. And these are just the trivial inconveniences of our traveling metaphor. Real life is much worse. Plans for a long and happy life are interrupted with terminal cancer, marriages are ripped asunder by selfishness and infidelity, crime victimizes and traumatizes us, wars claim the lives of our young men and women, friendships wither, children are abused, apartments burn down.

We may plan out life in a certain way, moving from Point A to Point B, always assuming that matters are within our control. They are not. We are sojourners in the midst of an unpredictable adventure, living with an illusion that the future can be domesticated when in fact it is filled with surprises, losses, adventures, pain, thrills, and struggle.

My friend Brent enrolled in a doctoral program so that he could become a psychologist and join his father's practice. He completed his four years of coursework, various clinical training placements, and his internship and residency; then, just as his dream was about to come true, his father died suddenly. Sitting at his father's funeral, I recall thinking how unpredictable and seemingly unfair life can be. The map is drawn: here is Point A, here is Point B, and this is how I get from A to B. Then floods wash out the road, and life is suddenly different. Though we might wish for a straight path through life, we all do our share of wandering, always looking for the safety and predictability of home.

The unpredictable adventure of life does not lead only to a series of losses and bad surprises. It also brings spontaneous joy and many good things. Rae, my daughter who is inclined to hitchhike, is also one who cherishes the adventure of life. She hikes and bikes in the woods, writes poetry, lives simply, stays up late to celebrate life with friends, and walks to a bridge in central Missoula almost every summer evening to stand amazed at the glory of creation as the sun rests once again behind western Montana's majestic mountains. As she was picking berries in the mountains recently, she realized that a pony-sized bear was standing beside her doing the same thing. So she made up a song about bears, stood very still, and sang her song quietly until the bear ambled off. Rae feels life, breathes it in, opens herself to the joy of each new day, and keeps her palms open to new possibilities. The adventure of life involves trials and troubles, but also brings great possibility.

If we are to find our way home in the midst of life's unpredictable adventure, it will be through the dark valleys of loss and the mountain peaks of spontaneous joy. We do not know what tomorrow will bring, but we keep moving on, daring to hope for the security of home and still inclined to venture out.

LIFE CONTAINS A DEEPER STORY

Hitchhiking is also like life in that it always has two stories. The first story is simple, perhaps simple enough to spray-paint on a cardboard sign. This story may simply be Toledo or Montreal or Seattle. But there is always a deeper story, something more interesting than what can be captured on a cardboard placard. The surface story is "Where?" but the deeper story is "Why?" Perhaps Toledo holds the promise of a new job or a new love. Maybe our symbiotic traveler chooses Montreal because it is far away from a painful past in San Francisco. Seattle may be a place of memories, calling a sojourner back home.

Even in *The Hitchhiker's Guide to the Universe* there is a "why" lurking beneath the vast "where" of space travel. In that story, the intergalactic travelers build a computer named Deep Thought to answer "the Great Question of Life, the Universe and Everything." It's a big question, so it takes Deep Thought a while to compute the answer—over seven million years. When the computer finally answers, it is disappointing. The answer to the Great Question of Life, the Universe and Everything is forty-two. This may not make much sense without reading the book, but it is reassuring to know that it doesn't make much sense after reading the book either. But even without understanding Adams's novel fully, I believe that he is describing our relentless quest to look deeper beneath the obvious story lines of our lives.

There is always a deeper story. It could be that someone has to hitchhike because her car ran out of gas on the freeway, or that a restless soul is yearning for the adventure of the road, or that a person cannot afford bus fare. There is always a "why" lurking beneath the "where."

Meet someone new and you will invariably ask one another what you do for a living. It's a fine question, likely to create interesting conversation, but it is only a question about the surface of life. You and I, and everyone we know and don't know, are persons of multiple stories. Perhaps you are an obstetrician, a homemaker, a clerk, a father of three children, a golfer, a student, a bridge player, a coupon clipper, a deacon, a carpenter, or a secretary. That story line, like the 10 percent of the iceberg that sits above the water's surface, says something important about you. But there is also a deeper set of stories constantly at work in each of our lives. Sometimes we become so compelled by our surface stories that we neglect the deeper motives and themes of our existence.

Early in my career as a psychologist I met with Tony and Lori, two successful middle-aged professionals, to help them with their marriage. After several months of slow progress, I recall Tony leaning forward in his chair to summarize his situation: "All my life I have wanted to be right where I am now.

I wanted to be successful, to have people admire me, to be on top of the world. And now I have it all. I have two Mercedes in the garage; I live in a huge, beautiful house; and I am a full partner in the most prestigious law firm in town. And it means nothing to me. I would give it all up today if I could have the happy life and stable marriage I thought it would bring." The passionate yearning in Tony's voice was heartbreaking. He was living the surface story portrayed in Hollywood fantasies, but it was all a glittering image, a counterfeit existence that befuddled his heart and distracted him from his deeper quest for meaning.

You and I are looking for something deeper than we know.

Tony needed to look for the deeper story. Raised as the only child of overachieving parents, he knew from an early age that he was headed to law school. He also knew that being second best was no better than being in last place. He kept pushing forward, trying to earn his parents' approval and love through unusual accomplishment. It worked. His parents were very proud. And it didn't work. Tony found himself in midlife tired and empty, depleted by a race with no finish line. It was time for him to look back, to connect the dots between past and present, to understand why he was working seventy-hour weeks and then feeling hurt and surprised when Lori did not admire him for it.

If we set aside the clutter of life and quiet ourselves long enough to hear the rhythm of our souls, we see that we are searching for something deeper than a promotion, something richer and more meaningful than another material possession, something more satisfying than entertainment.

LIFE CARRIES A CERTAIN VULNERABILITY

Hitchhikers are vulnerable—more vulnerable than they know. We read stories of hitchhikers being raped, robbed, or murdered, and mutter to ourselves about how foolish they are to put themselves in such a vulnerable situation. As I pleaded with Rae to reconsider her plans, I emphasized the danger and vulnerability of hitchhiking. She reminded me that we don't have to go thumb first to the closest freeway to be vulnerable. Life, like hitchhiking, is dangerous.

Perhaps every newborn should be branded with a Surgeon General's label: "Warning: Life can be hazardous to your health." We are prone to all sorts of problems throughout our days on earth, ranging from angina to brain aneurysms, from acne to posttraumatic stress disorder, from miscalculations to profound sins of betrayal. We are fragile creatures living in a fallen world, each of us more vulnerable than we know.

It is terrifying to see our vulnerability. So we don't look. Like hitchhikers, we close our eyes to dangers around us and naively hope for the best.

In 2003 *Newsweek* polled men about their health, asking how long they anticipate living. Of the respondents, 40 percent anticipated dying sometime before their eightieth birthday. Another 29 percent believed they would die before they turned ninety, 11 percent believed they would live into their nineties, and 10 percent expected to live past one hundred.[2] These men responded just as social scientists would expect, because most people estimate that they will live ten to twenty years longer than life insurance charts predict. The average life span for males in the United States is in the low to mid-seventies, yet most men think they will live into their eighties or nineties or hundreds. This is our invulnerability myth. We are more fragile, more vulnerable, than we are willing to recognize.

Similarly, we assume our marriages will defy statistics, our children will navigate adolescence without trauma, and our futures will be secure. We hold to our illusions of invulnerability in order to protect ourselves from the fearfulness of life and death—to avoid the harsh edge of truth. And when we honestly look at our fear, as I did in that phone booth by the Sunset Highway, the mere force of our emotions shocks us and makes us yearn for the security of home. We are vulnerable souls, constantly exposed to forces beyond our control, cloaked in fear, and shielded only by our illusions of control.

Being vulnerable seems bad—and in many ways it is—but it is also an impetus to search for hope and joy. Vulnerable people know they need something, know that their armor can never be thick enough, so they reach out to others, looking for help and refuge. If I had not felt vulnerable on that day in 1993, I would not have stopped at that pay phone, would not have reached out for Lisa's help, and would have missed a beautiful opportunity for connection with my lifelong lover. Sometimes we cover our fear and loneliness with grand plans and a frantic pace of accomplishment—symbolized on that particular day by my professional exam. When our fantasies of success are exposed as fraudulent and our vulnerability can no longer be hidden, then we glimpse the deep hunger in our souls that can never be filled by merit or effort. It is here in our brokenness that we come to our senses and reach out for another.

LIFE REQUIRES A LITTLE HELP
FROM OUR FRIENDS

This is another way hitchhiking is like life: hitchhikers cannot make it alone. Without the help of a compassionate or lonely driver and a functional car, hitchhikers would simply be hikers.

None of us can make it alone. We are created for connection, looking for love, yearning for attachment, always restless—as Augustine wrote at the beginning of his *Confessions*—until we find rest in God.

I suspect hitchhikers feel lonely sometimes, breathing in exhaust fumes along the side of a freeway, reaching out for help and finding so little. Even for those of us who have never hitchhiked, this picture of loneliness seems vaguely familiar, as if we also have stood at the busy places of life waiting to be noticed, looking for help, and sometimes finding so little.

Steve is a pastor—a good one. His parishioners appreciate his authentic preaching, his compassion for people, his care for his family, and his vision for the future. But Steve would tell you, as he told me in our counseling relationship, that pastoring can be lonely work. In one of our sessions—after working together for several months—I leaned forward in my chair and observed, "It must be difficult always being available for others, to care for their needs, and yet to feel that no one is noticing your needs." There are a few moments in almost every counseling relationship when some mystical connection occurs—as if the fuzziness of the world suddenly slips behind lenses that bring everything into focus. Tears welled in Steve's eyes; he sat silently for a moment and then affirmed, "That's exactly right. I feel so terribly lonely sometimes, so tired of giving to others, and I wonder when someone will notice my needs."

Steve was forty-five when he spoke those words, but if we listen carefully we hear the voice of the ten-year-old boy whose mother was terribly sick and unable to pay attention to her children. Steve longed for a home with a caring father and mother, but instead he had a disabled mother and a distracted father. When his mother committed suicide several years later, his father—overwhelmed with loss—sent Steve away to military school. He longed for home but was given a dormitory instead.

Sitting in my office thirty-three years later, Steve was still longing for home, yearning to be embraced and cared for by another. He had filled his life with the hope that serving others would cause them to care for him. Finally he was glimpsing how misguided his fantasy had been and how desperately he needed to find his way home. He could never fix what had been broken many years earlier, but he could begin to understand it, see the power it held in his life, and offer his broken past to God in anticipation of a day when Steve would truly be home in the presence of one who loves unconditionally.

Steve discovered in counseling that he needs others to care for him, laugh with him, pray for him, and journey with him through life. Though the particulars of our stories may be different from Steve's, we are all like him. We journey alone, and we all need others.

LIFE INCLUDES A HOMING INSTINCT

The other thing about hitchhikers is that most of them think about home while they're away. We venture out, sometimes searching for adventure and meaning and sometimes trying to mask our loneliness and fear. Some of our adventures are freeing and spontaneous and filled with delight, and some are rebellious forays into the prodigal's world of wanton carnality. But whatever sort of journey we are on, and whatever proportions of virtue and vice are part of the journey, deep in our beings we eventually sense a calling to settle back into a place of secure love. A hitchhiker may run as far as the highway system allows, looking for freedom and peace and possibilities. But sometime later—maybe a few hours or a few decades—home calls the hitchhiker back. So it is with life. The roots of home grow deep and cannot be cut off by moving to a different location or choosing not to think about the past.

Stories circulate about dogs who miraculously find their way home from great distances. Some insist the stories are true—that dogs have an innate homing instinct. Others see the stories as some combination of lore and coincidence, and point to the fact that many lost dogs roam streets and fields until their lives are claimed by searching owners, animal control workers, or speeding vehicles. Do dogs have a homing instinct or not? Because I am not a dog lover, I have suggested—only partly in jest—that we settle the controversy by taking our family dog to Connecticut, dropping her off, and seeing if she finds her way back to Illinois. Others in my family did not think this a very good idea, so we haven't tried my experiment.

Our human homing instinct is not like the instinct attributed to dogs. Most of us could find our way from Connecticut to Illinois with the help of a map, a thumb, and some good hitchhiking fortune, but that is because we have learned navigational skills rather than because of any innate instincts. Still, there is something innate to be explored here, and it can be seen both in human relationships and in the quest to know God. Think of the last time you quarreled with someone you love dearly—a spouse, child, friend, or parent. After the anger and irritation subsided, wasn't there some inner urge to come back together, to work out your differences, to live happily ever after? This is our homing instinct, to make peace with one another in secure relationships.

Contemporary psychologists speak of attachment theory, which posits that humans instinctively know to connect with one another. From the early moments of life infants are programmed to connect with their caregivers, and we seem never to outgrow that programming. Our longings for attachment follow us to school and the workplace; they come with us to the neighborhood park and into online chat rooms. And they call us to places of worship.

Perhaps we see our homing instinct best in the spiritual journey. None of us has seen God, yet we are called by the promise of secure love into a relationship with the divine. Our homing instinct to draw closer to God is strong, yet in so many ways we seem not to follow it, and even to subvert or contradict it. The fact is that we are frail, prone to sin. We fall down, sometimes over and over again, and each time we choose whether to give up or to struggle back to our feet and head toward home, toward God, once again. Two spiritual leaders of our time—C. S. Lewis and Richard Foster—give the exact same advice for people like us. It is surprising counsel. They say, "Never mind."

Lewis writes, "Never mind. After each failure ask forgiveness, pick yourself up, and try again. Very often what God first helps us towards is not the virtue itself but just this power of trying again."[3]

Foster writes, "we sin; we fall down, often—but each time we get up and begin again. We pray again. We seek to follow God again. And again our insolence and self-indulgence defeat us. Never mind. We confess and begin again . . . and again . . . and again."[4]

God always welcomes us home with open arms, regardless of the paths we have traveled, the dead ends we have pursued, the weary miles we have wandered, the number of times we have failed. God just wants us to come home.

3

Turning

You already know about an important phone call I made in 1993, but to understand the meaning of that call you need to know more. I write this chapter during the month of my twenty-fifth wedding anniversary. Sometime next week I will be hiding twenty-five roses throughout the house—some of them dark chocolate, some of them botanical, and some of them painted on the Franciscan Desert Rose stoneware bowls that will surprise Lisa and replace the seven bowls broken in a freak accident while entertaining guests almost a decade ago.

In some ways ours is a fairy-book story. I was the recipient of Lisa's first romantic kiss, and she mine, sitting beneath a huge evergreen tree nestled in the familiarity of a soft Oregon fog on a June day before our fifteenth birthdays. Tears well for the joy of knowing this partner of mine for so many years, for the faithful and steadfast people we have known who, like that evergreen tree, have shielded us from the harsh elements of life. I am grateful for the gift of touch that made feeling her lips with mine a sensual delight and still does to this day, for the gift of memory to keep that kiss locked away in our minds forever, for the tens of thousands of kisses that have followed over these many years, for the wrinkles that have begun lining our faces (mine more than hers), reminding us that we are growing old together, for the smiles and laughter, for the children who have blessed our lives, for countless dinner conversations, shared popcorn at the movies, walks to get Mama Sue's ice cream and Starbucks coffee, strolls around Lake Ellyn, for worshiping side by side week after week.

But we haven't always hidden roses around the house or delighted in each other with such joy. I remember a season of bitter acrimony preceding that 1993 phone call. Perhaps it is euphemistic to call it a season; it lasted four years or more, and it seemed like forever. Our lips stiffened, our wills hardened, our backs arched in conflict and disagreement. We said things we should never have spoken. Lisa was sure the conflict was my fault. I was sure it was hers. Day after day we marched along, unenthusiastic about our marriage but committed to the task.

Then came the lowest point of all—a dismal winter night in 1991 when our arguing awakened our three daughters. They congregated in a basement room with blue carpet and bluer parents, frightened and vulnerable little girls trying to make sense of a world that seemed to be falling apart. Even then, seeing the pain in the eyes of these precious children, I managed to keep to my hard-hearted conclusion that the conflict was Lisa's doing and not mine. I remember driving away that night, looking for a cheap motel, thinking that solitude was my greatest need and my only hope.

Although I found the motel, I never made it to the lobby. Inside the cramped quarters of a red sports car—one that I now realize signified something impulsive and reckless about me—I screamed out to God for answers to questions I could not even articulate. My life was replete with the markers of middle-class success, yet I felt profoundly lonely, isolated, and misunderstood. I was running from my pain, sitting beneath a neon motel sign pondering the meaning of my life.

When it seems we can go no lower, when the pain and struggle of life leave us breathless and bewildered, God often chooses to break the silence and speak truth into our frail lives. The Prodigal stood knee-deep in pig slop when he came to his senses and began to perceive his heart's leaning toward home. I sat waist-deep in self-pity, having filled my life with too many popular psychology books and entitled fantasies of what it meant to be loved unconditionally. Slowly I began coming to my senses. I eventually reached for the ignition and headed along Hillsboro Highway toward home.

It was a twenty-minute drive back to the house, but a much longer journey home to a place of secure love. Lisa and I had a good deal of work to do, and it took us many months to fully understand and begin recovering from our dysfunction. Each of us was partly wrong—and partly right—and we needed the help of a therapist to sort things out. In the process we sought and granted forgiveness, and we reclaimed some of the mystery of young love that had expressed itself under an Oregon evergreen many years before.

By 1993 we had healed to the point that I knew to call Lisa from that pay phone on the Sunset Highway. Her kindness in response to my cry for help moved us further in our healing journey.

In describing these memories I am humbled and saddened, yet also drawn to gratitude. I am grateful for second chances, for the cleansing power of God's grace and human forgiveness, for children who recovered as well as anyone could recover from such a thing, for the joy of reclaimed love, for the hope of living another twenty-five years with this partner of mine, for the truth that slowly seeps in as I see once again that God delights in redeeming us from the clutches of despair and rebellion. I am grateful for a God who brings us to our senses in the dreariest moments of life. Blessing and honor and glory be to God, now and forever more.

Embedded in this story is a motion: I turned from one direction to another, from nursing my anger and bitterness back to a place of secure love. This is a familiar motion for most of us because we make these turns throughout our lives. Turns toward redemption bring us back to a journey that is uniquely our own yet also is part of some bigger journey that millions of others have taken through thousands of years. It is a journey of faith and divine revelation just as surely as it is a journey of wisdom and human discovery. Life calls us to venture out, to take risks, to go outside the safety of things predictable, yet it also calls us to keep remembering the places from which we have come and the direction we intend to be heading.

As Lisa and I were turning back toward one another in the early 1990s, I began contemplating the various ideologies of our day and recognizing how many of them contain a redemptive language of turning back. Three of these ideologies—psychology, theology, and spirituality—have captured much of my professional attention since that time. In 1996 I published *Psychology, Theology, and Spirituality in Christian Counseling,* which seemed to me a preliminary pondering of how these three ideologies fit together. To my surprise the book has become a textbook in many undergraduate and graduate programs and brings with it various invitations to speak at interesting places around the world. Each time I prepare, travel, speak, and interact with students and colleagues, I feel nudged a bit closer to fluency in these three languages. Though not yet completely fluent, I find that each of these languages speaks of a turn toward places of secure love.

THE LANGUAGE OF PSYCHOLOGY

Psychology is a young science, still in the midst of what philosophers of science consider pre-paradigmatic fumbling. Whereas most well-developed sciences have a clear set of theoretical presuppositions, psychology is still an amalgam of competing worldviews and theories. And yet psychology is a surprising success story. The growth of psychology over the past century is staggering, both in terms of popular interest and the growing number of professional psychologists available to help people through the quagmires of life. The popularity of psychology suggests that psychologists are speaking a timely language that is relevant to contemporary society. Perhaps this is so because psychology helps us understand our yearning for places of secure love.

Claire's Got Rhythm

Jeremy, one of my doctoral students, brings his delightful ten-month-old daughter, Claire, to our research meetings. Claire crawls about the office as Jeremy and I talk. She explores the books on my lowest shelf, occasionally pulling herself up to gaze at the unreachable second shelf. She tugs at my file cabinet drawers, fumbles with the colorful plastic toys her dad provides, investigates the shiny metal base of the table where Dad and Dr. Who-knows-his-name sit (the one who makes funny faces trying to get her to smile). Claire is exploring her world—a world that will soon include the second shelf and will then grow at an exponential rate for the next couple decades. But Claire does something else, too. Every few moments she turns to look at her dad. If he is still there, then all is well. But if Jeremy has stepped into the next office to pick up a page off the laser printer and it's just Claire and Dr. Funny Face in the office, then Claire's face and spirit quickly rumple and she begins to make the sounds that infants make when trying to reclaim a parent. Jeremy returns, and once again life is good.

Here in the most ordinary psychology of everyday life we see the notion of a turn toward redemption. Claire is venturing out, her hitchhiking spirit emerging while she is still in diapers. But like all healthy infants, she periodically turns back to center herself in a place of secure love. Once re-centered, she goes back to the important work of exploring her world. Every now and then I also see Jeremy turning to look at Claire, not so much to see if she is getting in any trouble but to reconnect with the love she so simply offers him.

Venture out. Turn back to places of secure love. This is Claire's rhythm, just as it is Jeremy's and yours and mine.

Claire turns to see that her parent still loves her, and you and I do too. And this rhythm that we learn in early childhood spreads through all our lives as we turn to find secure love in the here and now. So I celebrate anniversaries and think about a first kiss under an Oregon evergreen and remember a phone call in 1993. Clinical psychologists often spend time with people for whom this rhythm has failed. Perhaps a parent did not love well or did not know how to express love in ways a child could receive it, or maybe the rhythm worked well in childhood but has sputtered later in life.

When the Rhythm Fails

One of my former clients was raised in a dangerous and unpredictable home. Tina could be slapped by her father one moment and hugged by her mother the next, or vice versa, without understanding what she did to evoke either response. Her uncle sexually abused her, and no one seemed to care enough to protect her. She felt confused, disoriented, unsure how the world works. Over time these feelings of confusion settled into a general attitude, a way of looking at the world. Psychologists call it a *schema*. Tina's schema told her the world is dangerous and unpredictable. This was true enough in her childhood world, but when she grew into adulthood her circumstances changed. Tina met and married a stable man, had three children, and later completed college and got a job she enjoyed.

But even in her new world, surrounded by successes, Tina's old schema still caused her to perceive the world as dangerous and unpredictable. She became unduly suspicious of her husband, chaotic in her parenting style, unpredictable in her new job. She viewed her adult world as if it were her childhood world, even though the circumstances were entirely different. Tina's story illustrates how crucial it is to experience places of secure love early in life. My job as a therapist was to provide a temporary place of security for her, to help her learn and apply to her current life the rhythm that comes so naturally to Claire.

Another person might have difficulty learning Claire's specific rhythm because of being raised in a "perfect" home, one where the reputation of the family is more important than personal connection. Anything that is imperfect must be kept secret because the family must be protected at all cost. Because our childhood schemas do not end when childhood is over, adults from these "perfect" families of origin still struggle to be open and honest with themselves and others years after leaving home. The pattern is passed from one generation to the next. Frederick Buechner provides a poignant and compelling look at the myth of a "perfect" family in his book *Telling Secrets* when he describes how his father's suicide was shrouded in silence both inside and outside the family. Dysfunctional schemas from our childhoods lead to many of the problems and challenges in our present experiences.

The language of psychology calls us to understand the places of secure love in our lives, and the times we may have wished for secure love but did not find it. With some practice and coaching, most of us can draw a continuous line between past and present and then glimpse where the line is pointing into the future. When we remember how things were, we can build a future that is deeper and richer because we have been willing to turn and look back. Psychotherapy is a place of secure connection that helps people gain insight into the past and resolve those inner conflicts that have been buried by secrecy and shame.

After going through psychotherapy himself, Buechner described the process of discovering the past: "The sad things that happened long ago will always remain part of who we are just as the glad and gracious things will too, but instead of being a burden of guilt, recrimination, and regret that make us constantly stumble as we go, even the saddest things can become, once we have made peace with them, a source of wisdom and strength for the journey that still lies ahead. . . . If this kind of remembering sounds like what psychotherapy is all about, it is because of course it is, but I think it is also what the forgiveness of sins is all about—the interplay of God's forgiveness of us and our forgiveness of God and each other."[1]

THE LANGUAGE OF THEOLOGY

Buechner seems to be suggesting that the language offered by psychology overlaps with some other language that is bigger, richer, more complete in scope, more powerful in its ability to explain issues of ultimate meaning. Theology—the study of God—provides a time-honored language that goes back many centuries before contemporary psychology.

God created us to be safely nestled in Eden, spiritually centered and whole. But God also made us to be adventurers, granting us minds and wills and hearts for going forth. So, perhaps paradoxically, we are both homebodies and pioneers, straining to discover the world yet built to find our way home.

Christian theologians begin with our creation in the image of a relational God, which means we are instinctively inclined to build families and friendships, to reach out in our vulnerability, to sojourn alongside others. In our human relationships we see a mirror of God who is divinely relational. We find our greatest joy in relationship because, as Buechner suggests, "we have God's joy in our blood."[2] This blood of ours calls us to human community—to the structures of family and friendship we construct—and, even more, it calls us to God.

But being home with God and one another is not so easy. In the biblical story of creation, when the Garden was tainted by sin, God sent Adam and Eve away from their perfect home with the warning that their hearts would linger in Eden. They had fallen and were exiled into a broken world. Adam was destined to toil, to fight the weeds, to wish for the way things used to be. Eve's curse was that she would long for Adam, for the full partnership and deep intimacy they shared in the Garden. Whether we take this literally or as a metaphorical love story demonstrating God's love for fallen humanity, we see that all of us are destined to pine for a home we instinctually know while we sojourn in some other place. Inclined as we are to run to faraway lands and squander our God-given resources, God always waits longingly and patiently for us to come to our senses and return.

What does it mean to be far from our home with God? There are countless ways that this theology is manifested in our lives. For Brian, once a responsible money manager, it is an addiction to phone sex that leads him to squander his money on 900 numbers. He longs to break the grip of his addiction, to stand faithfully and honestly before God.

For Melissa, who was badly mistreated as a child, it means she languishes in painful memories of abuse and wrestles with the daily burden of depression. Intuitively she knows that things are not right, that this is not the abundant life she seeks, yet the burdens of the past are heavy and her companions few. Melissa longs for home in the midst of a broken world, for a spiritual friend to guide her to a place of hope and light.

This is Stephen's theology, too. Laid off from his job, self-critical because he is not providing for his family, and wearied by the longstanding tensions in his marriage, he feels emotionally battered by a critical spouse and hassled by impatient creditors. As a child he dreamed of being a fireman or a Detroit Tiger or an astronaut, but never of being an unemployed auto worker. His dreams are withering even as he reaches out for help.

Life is tough—sometimes tougher than we may have ever imagined. We wonder how it could be this way. How could God be all-powerful and all good yet the world be so terribly broken? We limp through life with doubts and uncertainties, grasping for faith and sometimes finding so little. We wander in the wilderness awaiting the Promised Land.

All creation has been subjected to the effects of sin. Our motives are confused, our hearts crooked, our wills distorted. And we have been wounded by others who are equally confused, crooked, and distorted. Things are not right, and they have not been right for a very long time. Of course it is easy to see this in others and much more difficult to see it in ourselves. But the truth is that all of us are messed up, broken in various ways, and blinded to our own sin. We wander, thinking we will find something that quenches our parched souls, and instead we end up more broken, confused, and lost than we were before. In our hearts, we feel the desire to turn back toward God, even as we wonder how to find the way there.

One of the most tragic parts of my work is seeing people move in the wrong directions in their unhappiness. And this tendency is not limited to psychotherapy clients—we all tend to do it. We feel unhappy. Perhaps family relationships are not going as well as we want, or work has become mundane, or we suffer with a medical problem. Whatever the cause, in our unhappiness we search for ways to become happier, or perhaps just ways to soothe ourselves in the midst of life's pain, but often our searches lead us into places of greater rebellion and self-deceit. Before we know it we are knee-deep in materialism, or clenched in the jaws of an addiction or an illicit relationship, or clinging to mindless forms of entertainment that further numb us to the truth. Our quest to find happiness ends up bringing greater unhappiness.

If it were not for God's love we would be forever stuck in this vicious cycle, looking for love in all the wrong places. But in the presence of a loving and active God, we are surrounded with hope. God is in the business of redeeming—pursuing us, loving us, offering forgiveness and discipline—turning us back from our wanderings. God does not wait passively for us in the distance, but rather creates us with a desire for home and comes constantly and eagerly toward us when we are still a long way off. God pursues us.

God's redemption also has a future tense. We call it heaven because we don't yet think of it as home. But someday we will.

THE LANGUAGE OF SPIRITUALITY

The language of theology gives us the big picture of God's role in our lives, helping us keep our minds clear and our thinking straight. Sound theology is essential to keep us on track, but theology alone is not enough because it only provides knowledge *about* God. Theologian J. I. Packer writes, "interest in theology, and knowledge *about* God, and the capacity to think clearly and talk well on Christian themes, is not at all the same thing as knowing him. We may know as much about God as Calvin knew—indeed, if we study his works diligently, sooner or later we shall—and yet all the time (unlike Calvin, may I say) we may hardly know God at all."[3]

In his classic *The Great Divorce,* C. S. Lewis chronicles a busload of hell's residents as they visit heaven for a day. In a most poignant conversation, two former theology colleagues—one now a resident of heaven and the other a resident of hell—discuss the gulf between their beliefs. As the theologian from hell argues for the importance of scholarly inquiry and open-mindedness, his former colleague muses, "We know nothing of religion here: we think only of Christ."[4] If Christian theology is to be alive, it must be about knowing God as well as knowing about God.

Spirituality, informed by Christian theology, refers to the experiential aspects of our faith. It is knowing God, and it is worth at least as much as knowing about God—perhaps more. If theology contributes to head knowledge, then spirituality gives us heart knowledge of God. Our hearts need to be cleared and aligned at least as much as our heads.

Spiritual leaders throughout the centuries have used the metaphor of journey to illustrate the spiritual life. The thing about journeys is that they always have a beginning and a destination, and the two are related. We would not begin a journey unless we had the hope of a destination, and the only way to get to the destination is by beginning the journey. In Christianity the spiritual journey begins with an initial awakening, when we glimpse the destination. The mere possibility of finding rest in the embrace of a loving God inspires us, gives us hope and stamina, and causes us to seek truth. The Christian journey begins and ends because we hope to find our way home, and the promise of home gives our spiritual journey meaning.

In our fallen world, we sojourn between beginning and end, between our awakening to God's love and the ultimate comfort of heaven. This world is a broken place, so our progress toward spiritual wholeness is also broken. Along the way we stumble over our sin and the sins of others, we falter and doubt and struggle and strain, but with God's gracious help we can keep journeying with the hope of home on the horizon. With our eyes on God and our destination in mind, we find God turning our "mourning into joyful dancing" (Psalm 30:11).

At the risk of oversimplifying, I draw a distinction here between Christian spirituality and the many other spiritualities that have become popular in recent times. It seems that many of the spiritualities are about finding ourselves or ridding ourselves of effortful thought, looking inward to define the journey. Home becomes some state of inward repose and peace. From the perspective of the Christian spiritual journey, this is partly right—we certainly do find ourselves and empty ourselves and discover a good deal of peace through the journey toward God. But Christian spirituality is very different in that it begins and ends outside ourselves. Home is not merely an inner state of peace but a relationship of secure love with a transcendent God who loves us first, pursues us, draws us close. When we Christians "find ourselves" it is precisely because we are no longer trying to find ourselves. When we "empty ourselves" it is because we are no longer trying to empty ourselves, but are instead focusing on the transcendent God in whose image we are made. And, paradoxically, as we focus on our majestic and loving Creator, we find ourselves and empty ourselves and discover incredible peace at the same time.

Again I am reminded of baby Claire. She explores my office for treasures and then turns to find her father. I don't sense any frantic need for Claire to find herself. It is enough to explore and to remember that she is the beloved child of her father.

But I also know that life is simple for Claire. She lives with loving parents who care for her every need, and her ten months of life have not yet brought her to places of deep despair and struggle. Claire's story may remind us of the rhythm—exploring, then turning back to a place of secure love—but her journey is just beginning.

We long to find our way back to God, yet we struggle to do so. It is like one of those dreams in which you are running to get somewhere wonderful or to get away from something terrifying, but no matter how fast you run or how hard you try it seems impossible to make much progress. But still you keep running. And so it is with the spiritual journey. We keep trying to find our way home.

In one of his spiritual memoirs Frederick Buechner described a dream about a beautiful room, called Remember.[5] The name is fitting because we are called to remember our homes, to look back. And in remembering, we are also called to see the blessings of today and anticipate the great hope of the future. Buechner writes that in "the innermost heart, at the farthest reach, of our remembering, there is peace. The secret place of the Most High is there. Eden is there, the still waters, the green pastures. Home is there. I think our best dreams are always trying to move in that direction—homeward."[6]

Sit quietly. Breathe deeply. Listen.

Do you remember? Do you hear home calling? What keeps you from daring to dream about finding your way back?

PART TWO

Looking Back

4

Choosing to Remember

I have a love-hate relationship with my dentist. On the one hand, Dr. Davis seems like one of the nicest human beings on the face of the earth. He has a cheery smile and a remarkable capacity to remember details about my family, he tells good stories, and he is knowledgeable and competent. And I like his work. It's wonderful having clean teeth that rarely hurt, and even a custom-made mouth guard to keep my molars from cracking when I play basketball. I love the idea of avoiding the dentured life that my grand-parents' generation had to endure. In all these ways I am delighted with my dentist.

On the other hand, there's that movie I once saw in which a dentist was murdered. When the lead character found out about his dentist's tragic death, his first response was, "Oh, I would love to kill a dentist." This, of course, is a horrendous and awful thing to say, but I must admit to laughing a bit. My spontaneous laugh emerged from the things I dislike about dentists.

The first is their deplorable tools that drill and grind and demolish. As an amateur carpenter I have nothing against power tools, but all my primordial instincts tell me they should be kept away from my mouth. It is bad enough to deal with the high-pitched hardware moving in and out of my mouth, but it is doubly difficult to be a psychologist with a conversational dentist. We psychologists are trained to respond when others speak. Say something to a psychologist and you will get a reply: "Oh, that sounds difficult" or "That seems important—tell me more about it" or the standard paraphrase-and-repeat rhetoric. To be unresponsive when someone speaks is to violate years of psychological training and the rules of basic human civility.

So picture the situation: I sit in the dentist's chair; the dentist's latex-gloved hand, a stainless-steel clamp, and a gyrating power tool are all in my mouth along with a suction device and the latest polymers; and Dr. Davis is telling me stories about his child's boy scout troop, his days in the research lab, and the latest managed care scandal. Every instinct tells me to respond, to be an active listener, but all I can do is grunt and wonder if slobber is creeping down my chin.

Nevertheless, love him or hate him, I choose to schedule appointments and pay money to see my dentist twice a year. I know that going to the dentist is better than not going to the dentist. I choose to value the things I love about dental care more than the things I hate. Or, to put it another way, the consequences of not getting dental care are more dismal than whatever temporary discomfort I experience in having an occasional power tool in my mouth. And with time my choices have become habit, so going to the dentist is now part of life's routine—like flossing before bed or shaving in the morning.

To remember can also be a choice. There is both comfort and pain in looking back—things to love and hate—and some people choose not to remember in order to avoid the immediate discomfort of fear or shame or sadness. Looking back is untidy and inconvenient, reminding us that forgiveness is more a lifelong journey than a simple decision. It sometimes leads to the shadows of our lives where we are bombarded with conviction, remorse, and sorrow. But if we are wise, we push through the discomfort and choose to remember, knowing it is ultimately much better than not looking back.

HEALING AND REMEMBERING

Remembering is a natural part of psychotherapy, as it is with all forms of personal and spiritual formation. This is part of what makes us rational beings; we look back and remember the early days, thinking about the world we knew and the roles we played. We contemplate the times of grace, the warm embraces of acceptance, and the hope of deep and meaningful relationships. We consider how and what we learned to fear, grasp the bitter sadness of early loneliness, remember the pain of words that should never have been spoken, recall the stench of betrayal.

As we look back we begin to see patterns. Yesterday's roles get replayed in today's relationships. We love and nurture those close to us because someone loved and nurtured us years before. Yet we also struggle to love well, and we behave in destructive ways, in part because none of us was loved perfectly. In our remembering we discover that early wonders still need to be celebrated and losses still need grieving. We

65

identify self-destructive patterns. Our need to be forgiven, and to forgive others, becomes palpable. And the threads of fear and loneliness run through it all, and always will this side of eternity.

A Cold, Steely Stare and a Cold Metal Stair

Occasionally I have seen clients who are difficult to like. Frank was one. He came because his boss had given him an ultimatum: go to therapy or lose your job. These are not the best circumstances for a strong therapeutic alliance. Frank seemed to view all of life as a competition in which he felt compelled to assert his dominance. Although Frank's boss valued his work, Frank's office was filled with shouting and shrill orders, infecting the workplace with tension and resentment. I was annoyed by Frank for the same reasons his boss was perturbed. It was Frank against the world. And—at least in Frank's mind—I was part of the world. Frank's cold, steely stare told me that he saw me and the process of therapy as foes to be conquered. I found him intimidating, uncooperative, overpowering, and domineering, and I didn't like him.

I have learned over the years that when I don't like a client it is usually because I lack empathy—a lack that comes from not knowing enough of the client's story. And so I nudged Frank in that direction, encouraging him to remember, to look back. He spoke tentatively at first, recounting the sanitized stories that strong men tell, but eventually he began probing the depths of his past. He began to tell the story of his home, and though it was a home he had hoped never to revisit, he eventually found that remembering brought freedom and hope.

On a chilly Midwestern morning in the winter of 1964, Frank awoke to the cold moisture of his own urine and the silhouette of his father looming over him. His only sibling, a brother, lay beside him on the mattress plopped atop the dining table of the family's trailer home. Perhaps it was the soundness of his sleep, or perhaps the insecurity of attending eight different elementary schools in four years, but whatever the cause, his bladder hadn't made it through the night, and Frank knew he was in big trouble. His father was a small man who compensated by being as tough as the nails he pounded in his work as an itinerant construction worker. No son of his was going to be weak. Enraged, Frank's father grasped him by the shoulder, yanked him from bed, and discarded him on the front stair of the trailer, slamming and locking the door behind him. There Frank sat, in his wet underwear, his shame, and nothing else. He sat. He shivered. He watched the snow fall. He dared not cry. Some minutes passed—Frank estimated about twenty—before the door behind him opened and his father ordered him inside.

Frank did not cry, of course, because his father had foolishly raised a son who was strong enough to hide his weakness. I writhed in sorrow—for a lost ten-year-old sitting in anguish on a cold metal stair in his wet cotton briefs, and out of conviction for once not liking this friendless man sitting before me.

Frank learned from his broken and bitter father to begin viewing everyone around him as rejecting and critical. He learned to strike out first so as to protect himself from being vulnerable. He projected the same rejecting spirit onto God and wanted nothing to do with faith.

How often we pull away from faith because the unremembered wounds of the past blind us to the relentless love of God. We confuse the often limited human love we've known with the limitless love God offers us. The heart of God cries out in pain as we sit on the cold metal stairs that keep us far away. God aches for us to remember, to turn and come home.

There is a mysterious power in unlocking the secrets of the past and choosing to look back. For Frank, remembering helped him see that the script he learned in childhood—a schema he once needed to endure—was no longer working for him. His childhood formula for survival was simple: "Only the strong survive. Be tough. Compete. Eat or be eaten." He needed this schema to make it through his childhood, but he had outlived it. Now Frank had become an isolated man trying to function as an adult in a world that is, by and large, quite different from what went on inside (and outside) his family's trailer home. Instead of placating a dominating father, he was now alienating people who might otherwise care for him. Instead of avoiding an angry parent, he was now resisting a God who longed to reach out in love.

Remembering the past was the beginning step of a transforming journey for Frank that ultimately freed him to begin rewriting his childhood scripts and to form deeper connections with others and with God. Frank's remembering also penetrated my cold heart and helped me begin caring for a man who hid his loneliness with toughness, just as his father before him had done. Beneath his antics of domination lived a vulnerable soul longing for love and connection.

Scripts

Of course Frank's story is more than a story about him. It is each of our stories. Most people have less traumatic upbringings than Frank, but every one of us learned scripts as children—rules that helped us adapt to our early environment—and some of those scripts don't work well today. Some of us, like Frank, learned that they must be strong to survive. Some learned to accomplish big feats in order to be loved, and today they work sixty-five-hour weeks trying to follow the formula. Some learned that they must always have others' approval, so they live in fear of displeasing someone close. Some learned to manage anxieties and fears by controlling everything and everyone around them, and now they feel unloved if a partner or friend acts independently. The rules we learned back then usually don't work well now, and unless we look back, we allow the old rules to continue governing our lives.

Paradoxically, it is what we fail to remember that holds the most power over us. We can evaluate our scripts only after we discover them. The painful things of the past are important to recall so that we can learn to free ourselves from their grip, to turn our deepest pains and most persistent struggles over to God. And the beautiful things of the past are important to remember too, because they free us to believe in the transforming power of love. Those who dare to believe that God loves and cares for them can do so because they have glimpsed love in relationships with others.

In writing about remembering the past, I have no intention of ascribing malice to parents and caregivers.

Psychotherapists have already fostered more than enough victimization thinking. Many of us—perhaps most of us—were raised by those who loved us as best they could and made innumerable sacrifices to raise us. Cherished memories, some measure of mental health, goodness and hope are the legacy of caregivers. But even the best homes and the best parents are shaped by the unremembered forces of previous generations, cultural realities, and the broken world in which every family exists. Understanding these forces requires us to look back.

I was raised by two caring parents in rural Oregon. They taught me the virtues of responsibility and work, the importance of worship, the value of resilience and persistence. My mother would have done anything to help me, and still would to this day. If psychologists are correct that the goal of healthy living is to love and to work, then my mother is among the healthiest of all humans. Her capacity to love, like her capacity to work, astonishes me. My father came from difficult beginnings—including the first four years of life in an orphanage—and somehow managed to pull things together well enough to be a successful professional and an effective father. He also was a hard worker, juggling a full-time job and the forty-five-acre orchard that surrounded my childhood home. Not surprisingly, I learned to work. At age five I was working in the strawberry fields, my mother and sister at my side. By age twelve I was driving a tractor, and by fourteen I was mostly responsible for the daily operations of the orchard each summer.

That was then and this is now, but I find that a straight line connects those times and the present. Many of my best qualities come from the work ethic I learned as a child: I am productive, industrious, responsible, competent, and punctual. Like my mother, I take on extra tasks to express love and care for others. And some of my greatest struggles have those same roots. I have difficulty relaxing and enjoying the gentle breezes of life. Often I micromanage or fail to delegate, preferring to "do it right" myself rather than trust someone else. I have difficulty believing God loves me apart from my performance, so embracing grace is the monumental struggle of my spiritual life. And sometimes I mask the feelings of pain in my soul by taking on more work to distract me.

I am grateful for the scripts of my childhood, yet I find I must constantly remember them in order to keep them from running amuck in my life. When I fail to remember, I become demanding and drive others away. It's quite a paradox. In childhood we learn a certain approach to the world that helps us draw close to others, and our greatest strengths often emerge from this way of approaching the world, but when we apply the same rules later in life—especially when we do so indiscriminately—they can have the opposite effect. Sometimes our greatest strengths become our most troubling weaknesses.

There is healing power in our remembering—power that draws us close to one another and to God. This is not just the work of psychotherapy; it is found in all close relationships. Friends sit in coffee shops and cafes all over the world and tell the story of their lives. By remembering, they disarm the explosive power of unspoken memories as they begin to see their own lives through the eyes of another. Looking back puts us in touch with our stories, helps us connect past and present, allows us to disentangle today from the scripts of yesterday, and frees us to face an uncertain future with self-awareness and confidence.

A TALE OF TWO NOVELS

One more thing should be said about dentistry. The reason we need dentists at all is that our teeth decay. Enamel thins and molars crack and dental caries rage. And if the rest of our organs were as accessible as our teeth, we would see that every part of us is doing the same—steadily crumbling under the relentless pressure of time. We need dentists, and we need to remember, because we are slowly dying. You and I have a choice to make now, before the death of these mortal bodies is complete—to look back or not.

Each of us exists within a relational story, and one of the most important things we can do in life and death is build bridges of reflection and continuity between the past and the present. If we do this well, it draws us close to others.

Ivan Ilyich

In his classic novel *The Death of Ivan Ilyich,* Leo Tolstoy describes an isolated man who has lived a disastrously unreflective and selfish life. Ilyich lived his life superficially, focusing on money and professional status while avoiding meaningful relationships. When his marriage was troubled, he simply skirted the problem by investing more in his career as a magistrate. He saw his children as a distraction and a bit of a nuisance. One gets the impression that Ilyich was running as fast as he could to stay a step ahead of the existential questions that chased him. And then he became ill—probably with pancreatic cancer—and was left to make sense of his pallid life. Even in the midst of serious illness he obsessed about his physical symptoms instead of working to understand or repair his shallow relationships.

In reading Tolstoy's novel I am left with the picture of Ilyich spending his final days stuck in the great descent of his life, journeying in a direction that had been established many years before. The crest that lay behind him—between him and his memories of the past—was unbearably painful. Remembering would have required him to face the emptiness of his choices, acknowledge his role in a dysfunctional marriage, and make a turn toward humble apology and the hope of secure love. When he dared to look back, to reclaim the nobler values that were once important, he could get only a faint glimpse over the ridge of his fear and selfish ambition. To remember would have been to trudge backward, face his mountain of regrets, stumbling on his shame as he went. Tolstoy writes, "And when it occurred to him, as it often did, that he had not lived as he should have, he immediately recalled how correct his whole life had been and dismissed this bizarre idea."[1] Ilyich used a familiar formula for coping: if the truth hurts, shut it off. He could not bear to face his past.

The valley in front of him—one that he could not avoid—was the valley of the shadow of death. Nothing about Ilyich's death looked like heading home to a place of secure divine love. Instead, he lived his final days in terror. He "cried about his helplessness, about his terrible loneliness, about the cruelty of people, about the cruelty of God, about the absence of God."[2] He looked for answers and concluded there could be none. And then Ivan Ilyich died, alone and frightened.

When Ilyich's death was announced to his acquaintances, they immediately began thinking about who would be promoted to fill his job and who would acquire his seat at the weekly poker game. His widow seemed more troubled by the financial consequences of his death than by the loss of her husband. Tolstoy demonstrates that living without deep relationships gives way to dying without them as well.

If we are to live and die better than Ivan Ilyich, if we are to be grateful and surrounded with love in the final moments of life, and if we are to see dying as the means of entering our best home ever, we must be willing to retrace our steps to find that remembering has more power in our lives than the fear of cancer or the sadness of saying good-bye.

Lyman Ward

Another novelist, Wallace Stegner, also gives us a character nearing the end of his life. In Stegner's Pulitzer Prize–winning novel, *Angle of Repose,* Lyman Ward is an aging historian with a debilitating disease. He faces his fading existence by looking back and recalling the context of his life. As he sits in his wheelchair, he ponders, "Before I can say I *am,* I was. . . . What if I *can't* turn my head? I can look in any direction by turning my wheelchair, and I choose to look back. . . . That is the only direction we can learn from."[3]

And Ward does learn. By looking back to his grandparents' generation he begins to make connections between past and present. He begins to see his own struggle with forgiveness by remembering his grandparents' painful marriage and his father's bitterness. He gains wisdom by looking back. Stegner explains that *angle of repose* is an engineering term used in digging a ravine. When the banks are constructed at the perfect angle of repose it means that the dirt and pebbles stop rolling downward. Lyman Ward's grandparents, and he himself, and presumably all of us are looking for an angle of repose in life. We yearn to find that place where discontent and perplexity stop rolling over us. And when we find our angle of repose it will be because we have looked back well enough to understand something of who we are and where we are heading.

The beauty of Stegner's novel is that Lyman Ward—a lonely recluse—not only learns about himself in the process of looking back but also reclaims the importance of relationships in his life. Remembering is not simply a cognitive exercise; it is deeply relational, and it draws us to places of security and connection.

What we learn from Tolstoy and Stegner and countless other novelists and philosophers and poets is not so much how to die but how to live. We can choose to turn humbly in the direction of the past to find meaning in the present and hope for the future.

What we learn from the Christian faith is that living and dying also have an eternal dimension, so remembering is not only a matter of building better relationships here and now. Remembering God helps direct our journey through this life and will ultimately guide us from this life to the next.

REMEMBERING GOD

Remembering is also a spiritual endeavor. In remembering we create space for God to meet us in our journey, and we allow our lives to be centered in the security of God's love.

Spiritual remembering easily gets smothered with the routines of daily living. We don't rise in the morning with the thought, "My plan is to forget about God all day," but as we tumble into bed at night we may find that we forgot to remember God in the midst of the day's many demands. We don't climb in our cars at rush hour with the goal of forgetting spiritual virtues, but when other drivers start swerving into our lane and honking their horns and waving selected fingers in our direction, we might easily forget our security in God's love. It seems so natural to charge ahead with the demands of life, tyrannized by our schedules and others' expectations, without stopping to reflect on the most important matters of life and death.

The spiritual life calls us to slow down and create space to remember God in the midst of our confusing lives. Today we see renewed interest in spiritual disciplines—prayer, fasting, solitude, meditation, silence, confession, corporate worship, and others. This reflects a desire to turn from the hurried and frantic pace of today's world and from the existential ache of living outside Eden.

In his acclaimed book *Celebration of Discipline,* Richard Foster describes how desperately the world needs "deep people." He doesn't mean that most of us are shallow or lazy or unintelligent. He is not saying we need to work harder, to write "Be deep" on our to-do list. Instead, Foster's words point us the other way—toward slowing down. We become deeper, more reflective when we contemplate, sit still, pray, meditate, or just take a nap. All these practices slow us down and help us be more present to God, ourselves, and each other. If superficiality is the curse of our age, then the antidote is not found in doing more but in doing less, or perhaps in moving beyond our vocabulary of more and less and finding another dimension to human experience that brings reflection into our daily routines and helps us find a spiritual center in the midst of life's scurry.

The spiritual life is not intended to be an ashen existence obscured by long lists of empty rituals, but a verdant life with built-in habits of remembering God. Spiritual writers refer to this as *centering*—finding their way home each day, each moment, to the secure love of God.

I have already confessed to liking power tools, especially those kept a safe distance from my mouth. One tool in my arsenal is a belt sander. A belt sander has two rotating cylinders that drive a loop of sandpaper in a circular motion. It looks a bit like a miniature Caterpillar track that rotates around moving wheels. Belt sanders work well because they provide a constant source of sanding friction with the sand paper always moving in the same direction (in other words, there is no back-and-forth or circular movement). The biggest challenge I find with my belt sander is keeping the sanding belt in the middle of the two rotating cylinders. The belt tends to slip to the right or the left, and it eventually slides off the cylinders altogether if I fail to stop and make the correct adjustments. So I end up sanding a bit, then stopping to center the sandpaper, sanding some more, stopping, re-centering, sanding, and so on. Sanding takes a long time, and my belt sander requires frequent re-centering.

Belt sanding is not a profound thing in itself—even for one who likes power tools—but it provides a useful metaphor for Christian spirituality. We slide off center, you and I, and we need to stop and center ourselves over and over again. Spiritual practices call us to remember, to be centered in God's presence.

In the midst of a hurried world, Christian practices help us return to center even though there are deadlines at work and bills to pay and children to taxi and all sorts of other distractions. The world tells us to speed up and step up and keep up. God whispers an invitation to slow down, to sit down, to center, to remember, to be bathed in grace and love and wisdom, to keep Christ as close as possible to the core of our lives. The Bible says Jesus came to bring abundant life; we find abundance not by doing more things but by resting in the center of God's love. As the time-honored Heidelberg Catechism teaches us, belonging to God is our great comfort in life and death.

So here we stand—decaying teeth, aging skin, hardening arteries, aching joints and backs and all—with a choice to make. Do we live life by slogans—seize the day, move on, let bygones be bygones—or do we stop and remember how we arrived at this day before trying to seize it? It is as writer and spiritual guide Henri Nouwen writes, "Choices make the difference. . . . We have very little control over what happens in our lives, but we have a lot of control over how we integrate and remember what happens. It is precisely these spiritual choices that determine whether we live our lives with dignity."[4]

Looking back through eyes of faith brings secure love to all who enter the embrace of God. We remember God, who has always been with us—through the bitterest seasons of despair and the sweetest times of shalom—and always will be. And here we find mystery, because any notion of remembering God is only the inside-out expression of the greater truth: God remembers us.

5

Being Remembered First

Professors labor over scientific and professional papers for weeks, being sure to double-check every statistical computation and eliminate all split infinitives. Then the manuscript is published in a scientific journal—always accompanied by a long academic title with a perfunctory colon in the middle—where it is read by five or ten people and then tucked away in university libraries where it is utterly forgotten. But still, it seems important to those of us who do this work (and those who hire us). I was working on just such a paper in the midst of an office littered with books and journals when the ringing phone shattered my concentration.

"Dad, where are you?" These four words got my attention. The first let me know that the call originated from one of the people I treasure most in the world. The next three told me I had let her down. Sarah had finished play practice and shown up on the designated curb at the appointed time, waiting as patiently as a teenager can wait, but her taxi driver (a.k.a. the absent-minded professor, a.k.a. father) had not shown up. So she had trudged back inside the school to the nearest pay phone and tracked me down at my office.

Normally this would not be considered a parenting catastrophe, but just a few weeks before, I had attended a workshop where the leader had us visualize a young elementary school boy waiting for his parents to pick him up after school. A long string of parents arrived in their minivans and SUVs to take their children home, but this little boy's parents were nowhere to be seen. One by one his peers were whisked away to the security of home, and eventually he was all by himself, slumped on a curb in front of the school playground, left to ponder his aloneness in a large and frightening world. When the visualization exercise ended, most of us felt deep sadness for this boy's experience. The workshop leader went on to discuss how important it is for children to feel valued and remembered by their parents.

So these four words, "Dad, where are you?" carried a good deal of weight on this particular day. I scurried out of the office, raced to the school, apologized a half-dozen times on the ten-minute drive home and then completed the dozen later that evening. What I really meant was, "Sarah, please don't become a mass murderer because of this."

Most of us have had the experience of being forgotten. Perhaps you are meeting someone for the second or third time, but the other person thinks you are meeting for the first time. Your spouse forgets your birthday. A friend forgets a lunch appointment. An employer forgets you are due for a raise.

If you are a person of Christian faith, you dare to believe that God does not forget you, ever, no matter what. The majestic Creator of everything and everyone knows and cares about our struggles, celebrates our victories, grieves our sorrows, and holds us in the almighty arms of love. God remembers us first, even before we can utter our first words of praise or a cry for help. And this is a deeply personal sort of remembering. It is not just that God remembers us as we might remember a phone number from childhood or a favorite toy. God remembers us, knows us by name, and chooses to love us.

Finding our way home to places of secure love involves looking back through eyes of faith, to the greatest story of all—a story of how God remembers.

THE WORD BECAME HUMAN

God spoke through Isaiah the prophet, pronouncing to a chosen people: "I, the Lord, made you, and I will not forget to help you. I have swept away your sins like the morning mists. I have scattered your offenses like the clouds. Oh, return to me, for I have paid the price to set you free" (Isaiah 44:21–22). Like the Israelites to whom Isaiah was speaking, when we are under the cruel bondage of slavery and in need of exodus, when former temples and city walls lie in heaps of rubble, when giants threaten to slay us, when despair and hopelessness surround us, when life makes no sense, when it seems that God is nowhere to be found, God does not forget us. This is the God who, like the Prodigal's father, woos us home, sees us from a distance, and comes running to embrace us and forgive us not only for straying but for all the wrongs we have done.

This all may sound so theoretical, so distant, so formulaic, so removed from everyday life. But it is not. It is arguably the most practical and tangible truth of all because God embodied this remembering in the person of Jesus. "So the Word became human and lived here on earth among us. He was full of unfailing love and faithfulness" (John 1:14). Each year Christians all over the world—and many who are not Christians—celebrate God's becoming human and living among us.

There was a time when I found Christmas annoying: the marketing flurry, the trite and empty platitudes about the "true meaning of Christmas," the life-endangering trips up the extension ladder to hang lights, the squandering of innocent pine trees, the superficiality of the season. Bah, humbug. And then something changed. It didn't take the Ghost of Christmas Future to change my views, but a class on incarnational theology—the study of what it means for God to become incarnate (literally, "in-fleshed"), to have taken human form in the person of Jesus Christ. For centuries the Orthodox Church has been celebrating the incarnation in ways that I, as a Protestant, had failed to appreciate. And it is of course what we are celebrating at Christmas. In this incarnational theology class I began to grasp the miracle of it. God becomes human. The divine and immaterial are bound up in the mortal and material in order to reach fallen humanity. God not only remembers but breaks in, bursts into human form, and lives with us—Emmanuel, God with us.

This mystery of the incarnation distinguishes Christianity from every other religion. Christianity is the only major religious tradition that says God came to us and lived as a human being, even experiencing human birth and death. God is with us, in our midst, in human form, facing temptation, getting splinters in his fingers and rocks in his sandals, weeping, feeling angry, hungry, and tired, suffering for lost humanity.

Emmanuel comes in flesh and bone, in vulnerability and tenderness. If our Christmas celebrations fill our senses with fresh sights, sounds, smells, and tastes, then rather than being grumpy about the extravagance of it all I should be marveling in the materiality of God's love. God remembers us—not just peering in on us from some faraway heaven but taking on matter, being confined to human form, and living among us. So let's deck the halls and let the hardiest lovers of Christmas start the festivities the day after Halloween. And I'll keep climbing the extension ladder to hang the lights that Lisa loves, because I am reminded by the incarnation that love is nothing at all if it is not made tangible. Sacrifice a young evergreen if you must, and adorn it with tinsel and bows and lights that flash in all sorts of colors and rhythms. Bring on the eggnog. Revel in laughter and family visits and the joy of good friendship. Wrap presents and stuff stockings and listen to silly carols about sleigh rides and Mommy kissing Santa Claus. And in all of these festivities, we remember Emmanuel, who remembers and is with us.

And when December 26 comes, when the lights are put back in boxes and the tree is hauled away and the bows are put in a storage bag so they can gild next year's presents, when the school holidays are over and families go back to their routines, when the Christmas cookies are all gone and it is time for New Year's resolutions, when the gifts are all dispensed, and when this year's Christmas begins its journey toward becoming another distant memory, we can rest in the assurance that God's memory—like God's love—never fades. In every season of life, God remembers.

RIPPLES OF THE INCARNATION

I love Christian theology for all sorts of reasons, but I am especially drawn to its relevance to the deep psychological realities of life. I must be cautious here, because theology is not intended to be psychology. Karl Barth, the renowned twentieth-century Swiss theologian, emphasized that theology is first and foremost the study of God, and not the study of humankind. We get into intellectual and spiritual quagmires if we begin reading Scripture as a psychology text. Nonetheless, Barth recognizes—and we should too—that those who study God also end up understanding something important about human nature.

We might think of the incarnation as a rock that falls into a lake. At the epicenter is the stark reality of God bursting into our broken world. But flowing out from the central truth of the incarnation are all sorts of human implications—ripples emanating from Bethlehem and touching every corner of creation.

If God is with us, it means that human understanding can be rooted in something bigger than an individual's life and ancestry. Looking back is not just a matter of contemplating our personal histories, recalling our childhoods, talking about past joys and trauma. Looking back is much bigger. In the darkest times of life, when there seems to be no light of hope to be found, we can look back to centuries gone by and reach out to the people of faith who surround us today and claim the truth that God is with us then, now, and always. Perhaps we claim such a thing only by faith because our ability to see God's goodness has been swallowed up in the present darkness, but what a miracle it is to have such faith. When I say "only by faith" it may seem to minimize its treasure, but to my way of thinking I could not hope for more in the darkest times.

Another ripple out from the central miracle of the incarnation can be seen in our care for one another. This may seem far-fetched, that a theological notion could transform how we relate to one another, but the reality of the incarnation can never be contained in theology books or pulpits. Because we see the boundless love and care that God showed in becoming incarnate, in living with us on this earth, we feel called to emulate that love and care in our relationships with our fellow human beings. From the time of Jesus to the present day, Christians have been active in establishing orphanages and homeless shelters and all sorts of humanitarian relief. Of course many people care for others regardless of their religious faith. One need not be a Christian to be a caring, helpful person. But I would argue that even this impulse is a ripple of the incarnation. God's character is revealed most fully in Jesus, but the rest of us—created in God's image—also reveal something of God's character. Whether we attribute it to God or not, we carry around some of God's personality, and so we reach out to people in their pain, sit with them, care for them, offer them comfort and encouragement. God, who loves us so much as to come be with us in our messy world, made us to be with one another.

Also rippling out from the incarnation is the invitation to reach out to Jesus for healing and hope. When Jesus walked the earth, crowds pressed in around him to see him, hear him, and touch him. No one knew then that Jesus was God incarnate, but folks intuited that there was something more about this rabbi, something that could heal them. One woman had been hemorrhaging for twelve years. She fought through the crowds, sneaked up behind Jesus, and dared to touch the fringe of his robe. Jesus sensed her presence, turned and said, "Daughter, be encouraged! Your faith has made you well" (Matthew 9:22). I wonder how many times in the preceding twelve years that woman of faith had prayed to God for healing. But here was someone tangible: a prophet, a healer—perhaps, she dared to think, the Messiah—and if she could just touch him she knew she could be healed. God remembered her, and you and me too. In the incarnation, God becomes someone who can be touched and whose touch can heal.

The incarnation has the potential to touch each of us in our immediate troubles. We all face troubles—difficult relationships, fear, anxiety, sexual struggles, financial challenges, sadness, and loneliness—but as we look beneath the symptoms and the unique circumstances of each human life we find a common human yearning to be esteemed, known, and loved. And Jesus speaks to us, "Daughter, son, be encouraged! Your faith will make you well." This is no trite spiritual cliché, but the timeless truth of God manifest in Jesus. The mystery of the incarnation—of God remembering and being with us—has the potential to soothe and even heal the sickness of the human soul.

TO BE ESTEEMED

Psychologists speak of self-esteem and have conducted thousands of scientific studies to demonstrate its importance for emotional health, but I sometimes wonder if there are more important aspects of human experience lurking beneath that concept. Perhaps we study self-esteem because it is relatively easy to measure with pencil-and-paper questionnaires and because most mental health professionals can agree on its importance. But self-esteem language can also be confusing, because decades of social psychology research demonstrate that most of us tend to overestimate our opinions and abilities. We tend to think too highly of ourselves. Those who really do suffer from genuine self-esteem problems have usually been wounded in previous relationships, which makes me wonder if so-called self-esteem problems are first an *other*-esteem deficit. It may help to teach people with low self-esteem to think more kindly toward themselves, but perhaps the deeper quest is for someone else to think kindly of them.

All of us want to be deemed important, to be esteemed and valued. It seems to be wired into our personalities. When children are raised without being valued by their parents they are almost always severely damaged as a result. Even those from relatively healthy homes where they received a good deal of attention seem to maintain a lifelong desire to be considered important. Much of life seems to be an effort to get others to notice and value us.

This struck me recently as I sat at a traffic light (a popular activity in the Chicago area). My window was down, and I listened to the sounds of a middle school track meet—public address announcer reciting names, coaches shouting instructions, students cheering on their peers. Without warning, I was flooded with memories. I thought back to my years of middle school and high school athletics and how much I wanted to be noticed and deemed important. Our high school football coach encouraged us to wear our jerseys to school on game days, and so in celebration of my supposed athletic prowess I learned to walk with a certain varsity swagger on those days: chest out, slight horizontal sway with each step, knees faintly bowed outward. No one warned me that the varsity swagger could become permanent. Even now, almost thirty years later, people tell me I walk funny, and I think it is because I cannot unlearn how I taught myself to walk back then.

On the football field, I played hard, hoping to help my team win the game. But I also played hard because I wanted the coaches to notice, to be impressed with my performance, and then to award me with one of the maroon football decals that adorned the helmets of the really good players. To be honest, I wanted more than just the coaches to notice and remember me. I wanted my parents to be proud, my friends to think I was tough. And I especially wanted the pretty girls to notice me so that the next time I swaggered down the hall they would say to one another, "Isn't that the football star?" I never was a star, though. I was a lineman, and linemen know nothing of stardom. So I had to work harder than ever to be noticed. Like when I would take off my helmet after a touchdown drive, prop it under my arm so that my few maroon decals would be noticed, and just hope that some of the pretty girls would think, "Oh, I know that guy. He's in my biology class. I like how he walks."

It seems different now as an adult, looking out the car window at the student athletes and realizing that what they are doing is much less noteworthy than they think. Like my high school football career, their performances in track and field are really quite forgettable, quite transient and unremarkable. We can slap self-esteem stickers on each student athlete and pretend that their capacity to run or jump or throw is what makes them important, but ultimately the stickers will be as unconvincing to the students as to the adults who provide them.

And then I looked around at all the other suburban folks sitting in their cars waiting for the light to turn green, and it occurred to me that we are no different than those middle school athletes. Here we are, still hoping to be noticed and remembered for the work we do, the car we drive, the way we raise our children, or the way we care for our bodies. We may not mark our successes with maroon football decals, but we have other markers: salaries, job titles, physical appearance, academic degrees, swanky addresses, and children's accomplishments.

Then I began thinking of all the thankless jobs in the world and how easy it is to treat people as if they are invisible. How many times do we encounter the checkout person at the grocery store or the clerk at the gas station without ever noticing the name printed on his or her badge? And how often do we gripe about being caught in traffic behind a garbage truck or a school bus without a moment of thankfulness for the men and women who are picking up our trash and driving our children home from school? I was jolted into a view of my arrogance. Sometimes I live as if my various attributes make me more important than those who have lives with less prestige. I wonder to what extent I did the same thing in high school, swaggering down the hall without giving a moment's thought to those who didn't or couldn't play football, or those who suffered invisibly with shyness or social alienation or with disabilities or illness. I deemed myself important because of a football jersey, and I expected others to do the same.

This may sound harsh, as if I am suggesting that neither student athletes nor middle-aged suburbanites nor those with invisible jobs are important. Not at all. The truth is that we *are* important—every one of us priceless masterpieces of God—no matter how fast or slow we run or how much or how little money we earn. God became flesh and dwelled among us, demonstrating that whether or not we have self-esteem, we are noticed and deemed important by the eternal Creator of the cosmos.

It seems difficult to rest in the truth that God deems us important—esteems us—without our having to do anything special to receive that love and valuing. There is no varsity swagger that can put us on God's "worth remembering" list. Logically, this also means we cannot cajole God into liking us through noble deeds or lose God's esteem because of our waywardness. It would be foolish to conclude that God doesn't care how we live, but it is equally foolish to think we can catch God's attention through our good or bad actions. We already have God's fond attention, and can never lose it.

In our Western individualism we can easily distort this idea to fit a narcissistic formula: "God deems you—*name*—important." By filling in the name—Ralph or Rasheed or

Rachel—each person can feel individually valued by God, receive a sort of personalized affirmation from the Creator, designed to make us happy. The more essential point is that God views *us,* collectively and individually, to be important. So it is not just that I am important or that you are important, but also the person living next door, the customer in the showroom, the convicted pedophile, the CEO and the assembly line worker, the telephone marketer who interrupts dinner, the person driving recklessly down the freeway. God deems us all important, and this is precisely the way we ought to view one another.

TO BE TRULY KNOWN

Being deemed important is poignant, but that is not all. One can be noticed, and even deemed important, without truly being known. For example, those of us who shop online are noticed. When I look for a book, I am greeted with, "Hello, Mark." The cyber-bookstore even recommends particular books I might like based on my previous purchases. My presence is noticed and remembered. I suppose I am even deemed important. Once a year or so I get a gift from this online bookstore, thanking me for my obsession with books and for choosing to spend way too much money at its Web site. But this sort of relationship with Amazon.com does not really satisfy my deep relational yearnings. They may notice me and consider me important, but only in a nonrelational be-sure-to-update-your-credit-card-information sort of way. It would be foolish to expect any more from an online merchant.

This is not the way God remembers and knows us. We are deemed important, to be sure, but we are also personally known and understood. The incarnation means that Jesus understands our struggles, because he lived in our midst. He knows what it means to be hungry and tired, to live alongside those who treat us unfairly, to yearn for understanding and justice and shalom. And we are invited to know God because Jesus is God revealed in human form.

To say that you and I can have a relationship with God is a phrase that has been largely spoiled by television evangelists with their constant question: "Did you know that you can have a personal relationship with Jesus Christ?" It seems almost automatic to follow such a statement with a toll-free phone number and a request for a generous donation to "support this important ministry." Although I have little doubt that these evangelists are right—indeed we can have a relationship with Jesus—I fear they often fail to capture the depth of this pronouncement. Their idea of a personal relationship with Jesus seems to have a particular spin that is more about staying out of hell than about knowing and being known by God; more about presenting ourselves with acceptable religious manners than pouring out the brokenness of our lives in authentic connection to Jesus, who understands our struggle and weakness.

Not long ago I heard a worship leader pronounce that having a personal relationship with Jesus means we will be filled with joy and will never again thirst for significance, meaning, or direction. Slowly, I slithered down in my chair, engulfed in shame, wondering why I feel so thirsty. Why do I still struggle with pride, fatigue, selfish ambition, lust, and greed? Why do good people suffer so? I wanted to hide from the God this worship leader described.

Then I remembered that the incarnation cries out against every shallow theology and simplistic formula ever spoken. Jesus dwelled among us. He knows what it is like to be tempted and tired, to face anxiety and fear—even to sweat drops of blood—and to hang on a cross and cry out, "I am thirsty."

With these words of Jesus I sigh in deep relief, because here is a God who understands far more than I do about what it means to be thirsty. Here is one who knows us and identifies with the struggles of life, who has experienced more pain and suffering than we can ever imagine. Jesus gets it. He is with us.

Sunday school children memorize John 11:35 because it is the shortest verse in the Bible: "Jesus wept." But it is also one of the most important. Jesus' friend Lazarus had died, and his family was suffering the deep ache of loss. And when Jesus saw what was happening, he started aching too. He was indignant with the futility and vulgarity of death, and terribly sad for the pain of human suffering. And he wept.

I have no need to hide from the God of the incarnation. I can pray to this God who knows and understands me. I can speak the truth about what I feel, when I struggle, how I fail, and when I encounter joy and victory. God is not shocked or surprised by any of it. Even if it were possible to hide ourselves from God, there is no need to do so. God knows us— every doubt and fear and longing.

And if God knows us and understands, then the incarnation opens the possibility of our living authentically with one another. We can tell people we are thirsty rather than slinking in shame because we don't always live abundant lives. We can struggle together in honest relationship, knowing God understands. Together we can look, really look, at the messes and struggles and pain of life and death.

I was reminded recently of the power of being known when I had breakfast with a friend of mine. Jeff and I had been friends for several years and had always enjoyed our conversations, but there was something different about this day. Our years of friendship had somehow made us feel safe enough with each other that, this morning at least, we went ahead into the unfamiliar and vulnerable territory of our fears. Jeff told me about his fears for his children, then he spoke of his uncertainties at work. Then, as I consumed my heart-healthy egg white whole wheat French toast and he ate his oatmeal, we spoke of our aging bodies and fears about health and premature death. I spoke of my fear of incompetence, my doubts about how I raised my children, my fear of disappointing others. I fear being fully known, I fear my sexuality, I fear failing even more than I fear succeeding. Jeff and I listened to one another. He understood in a way that good friends understand, and I think I understood him too. My friend was with me, and I was with him. If God is with us, knowing and understanding us, then we can be inspired by the incarnation to know and understand others. This is proper work of the body of Christ, the church, where we speak the truth, acknowledge the grime of living, and allow God to cleanse and grow us. As Jeff and I left the restaurant and headed in different directions, I felt a wave of peace wash over me. The unspoken terrain of my inner life had been spoken aloud to a friend who knows and cares for me. The terrifying things that lurk in my mind had been released, evaporating into the light and warmth of a new day. I had a human glimpse of a divine knowing and loving that I believe is fully lavished on me. If Jeff and I could be so much with each other, how much more can God be with me, no matter what?

TO BE LOVED

Our deepest longing in life is not merely to be known and understood, but to be loved, to be the apple of someone's eye. Greg, an eight-year-old whose words made it to the newspaper, put it this way: "Love is the most important thing in the world, but baseball is pretty good too." By age twenty-five, I doubt Greg will be thinking as much about baseball.

Just as my effort to reach out for secure love in the midst of a turbulent time led me to a phone booth on the side of the highway in 1993, all of us reach for love. In various ways our lives are marked, and even defined, by our quest for love and the fears that interfere. I recall coming across a sociology text on love many years ago and being both saddened and compelled by the author's introduction. He explained that the reason he studies love is because love has been his most illusive dream. Though he had spent his life searching for love, he had yet to find a deep, meaningful love relationship. He is not alone in his quest; we all search for love. Think of the movies and television we watch, the fiction we read, the songs we sing, the dreams we dream.

Love is sometimes nurturing and altruistic, as with the love an excellent parent offers a child. Other times it is very tangible and practical, expressed as shelter and a hot meal for someone living on the street. For some it is wildly physical, bringing two bodies together in sexual ecstasy. Others experience love as safety, as friends walking together through the valleys and over mountaintops. Sometimes it may seem that God's love is a faint consolation to all of these because it is intangible, seemingly distant and removed from daily life, but I believe—in faith—that in these moments we have it backward. God's love is at the center of everything, and the rest of these expressions are mere ripples of the greatest love of all.

Jesus had a follower, John, who was so confident in Jesus' love that he referred to himself as the "one Jesus loved." What a gift to have lived and walked with Jesus, to see God's love expressed in eyes filled with compassion, in laughter and playfulness, in words of empathy and comfort. John later penned words that have been repeated ever since in literature, poetry, and song: "perfect love casts out all fear." Fear is the enemy of love. In our fear, we scurry along trying to be good enough to earn love. Fear keeps us from sacrificing ourselves for the sake of another. What if no one notices? What if the other person doesn't appreciate it? What if I fall behind in my other responsibilities? Fear keeps us obsessed with aging as we confuse love with physical attractiveness and sexual desire. Fear prevents us from being authentic with others, blocking us from the depth of pure love. Our fear reveals that we are lost.

In the incarnation, God fully expresses his love, reaching down to lost humanity, offering to cast out fear. This is a love that violates all common sense, yet nothing makes sense without it. No word or picture can come close to describing this love, and yet it is—directly and indirectly—the topic of innumerable books, conversations, and pieces of art. This love transcends all boundaries of time and space yet touches us in every time and every place and was expressed most fully in great particularity—in a manger in Bethlehem and on a cross outside Jerusalem.

I began this book by defining home as a place of secure love, known most fully in the embrace of God. It is only after considering the incarnation that this definition begins to take on its full meaning. God's love is at the center of the home we long for, but this sort of love ripples outward too, blessing all sorts of relationships. So we find our way home to other places of secure love—to spouses, friends, parents, and children. Whether or not we acknowledge its source, God's love permeates all creation and provides many places of safety and rest. It all begins with the first love who remembered us, dwelled among us, and still to this day invites us to leave our fears behind and find our way home.

Nouwen expresses it beautifully: "Home is the place where that first love dwells and speaks gently to us. It requires discipline to come home and listen, especially when our fears are so noisy that they keep driving us outside of ourselves. But when we grasp the truth that we already have a home, we may at last have the strength to unmask the illusions created by our fears and continue to return again and again and again."[1]

6

Forgive and ~~Forget~~ Remember

My friend Everett Worthington is author of many books. One of the most powerful is *Forgiving and Reconciling*.[1] In the first chapter, Ev describes a most awful New Year's Eve on which his mother was murdered by two youths intent on burglary. The repugnance of murder is always unspeakable, but this was unimaginably awful—assailants splattering an elderly woman's blood with a crowbar and then penetrating her with a wine bottle. I would not usually dare reveal such personal information about a friend's tragedy, but Ev has already described the story in his book, so—with his permission—I include these gruesome details.

Before this horrifying event, Ev had already emerged as one of the world's leading experts on the scientific study of forgiveness, but now forgiveness was no longer about the ivory towers of academia, independent and dependent variables, and well-controlled research designs. Now it was personal.

In his book, Ev goes on to describe his struggle to forgive. He didn't want to forgive—it would have been much easier to cling to the rage and hate. And even if he wanted to forgive, he was not sure he would be able to. It is one thing to forgive someone for forgetting your name or making an insensitive comment, but how could one forgive such an immense offense as this gruesome murder?

Ultimately Ev chose the long, arduous path of forgiveness. Some would say that he should not have forgiven—that doing so would keep justice from occurring. Some have even suggested that forgiveness is cowardly. Ev disagreed: "Having faced a major hurt and struggled with whether to forgive, I can't buy that. For me, it's harder to forgive than to hate. It's not cowardly to want to give up the hatred that makes a person feel powerful (and makes us wish the perpetrator were weak). It takes courage to grant love that can help *both* people feel stronger and better as people."[2]

I see Ev two or three times a year at various professional meetings, and each time I see his gentle face my first thought is, "How is he choosing to forgive such an abominable offense?" Ever the scholar, Ev has conducted various scientific studies—both before and after his mother's death—to explain how forgiveness happens. I will leave the science to Ev, but forgiveness is also worthy of spiritual reflection in relation to finding our way home.

You and I have been wounded by others. God knows we have done our share of wounding also. We have been belittled, betrayed, discounted, discarded, and disregarded, and we—in our pain perhaps—have dished out much of the same fare we have received. Some of our wounds are small, like a tiny abrasion that heals in a few days. Others are deep and profound, like a life-altering injury that leaves one disabled for life.

Some would tell us to forget about it, to put the past behind us. This reflects a docile approach to healing and ultimately leaves us powerless and helpless. It is much wiser to wage peace, to engage in the long and arduous journey of remembering, celebrating joys and grieving losses, listening to our pain and learning from victories, recognizing our own sin, and ultimately moving toward the sort of healing that is costly and active. The path to peace and forgiveness is not found through forgetting, but through remembering. Nouwen writes, "If God is found in our hard times, then all of life, no matter how apparently insignificant or difficult, can open us to God's work among us. To be grateful does not mean repressing our remembered hurts. But as we come to God with our hurts—honestly, not superficially—something life changing can begin slowly to happen. We discover how God is the one who invites us to healing. We realize that any dance of celebration must weave both the sorrows and the blessings into a joyful step."[3]

PERSONAL REMEMBERING

The forgiveness that Everett Worthington describes in *Forgiving and Reconciling* is no passive task. It takes enormous work, and it requires a person to remember the agony he or she has experienced. Ev has developed a pyramid-shaped model for how the work of forgiveness can be done. In the first step of the pyramid model, we deliberately recall the hurt.

Feel the wound. Admit the pain. Acknowledge the fear the offense engenders, the anger it evokes, the secret desire for retaliation we nurse. Remember.

Another friend, Ray, has struggled with forgiveness for his prodigal father, who like his father's father, spent the best part of his life at the local tavern and had little left for his children. Ray remembers being a frisky eight-year-old child, frolicking about the front yard, tossing a baseball in the air and catching it in his mitt as his father sat idly on the front porch. Ray finally mustered the courage to issue an invitation he had never given before. "Dad, do you want to play catch?"

"No."

Then silence. Shame settled into his eight-year-old psyche. "It is you, Ray," he thinks. "You are bad. You are not loved because you are not good enough."[4]

The silence continued through Ray's formative years: silent tension around the dinner table, silent rides in the car, silent looks of disapproval, silent bouts of waiting in the passenger seat while his father stopped by the tavern, silent incubation of shame in a young boy's soul.

Eventually his parents divorced, and his father moved to an apartment two miles away where he lived for twenty-eight years before dying. Ray's father called Ray four times in all those years, three of them returning Ray's calls. He missed Ray's graduations: high school, college, and graduate school. He never spoke the magic words, "I love you," though once he was able to choke out, "I am proud of you."

In all these ways and a thousand more, Ray was wounded. He was robbed of the father-connection that brings life, abundant life, to children and young people and grown adults. I imagine he was tempted to bury those wounds deep in the recesses of years gone by, to forget the past and charge forward into the future. He could have channeled his anger and shame into relentless work, into competitive sports, into a demanding, controlling way of relating to others. But that's not what Ray did.

When Ray and his wife were expecting their first child he created enough space in his life to remember. He contemplated the question that haunts fatherless sons all over the world: "How can I become a father when I did not have a father?" Ray saw a counselor to help sort it out, sifting through excruciating emotions of loss and betrayal in the process. Forgiveness is never easy when the pain runs deep; pain forced Ray to look back at the ache of what he wished for and never had.

At one point, Ray recalls driving to a church parking lot after one particularly painful session so he could continue sobbing and pouring out to God the memories of his unfulfilled childhood. He writhed in anguish as he reflected on all the unresolved feelings of the past—his fears, anger, sorrow, and longings. This was not tidy contemplation. It was full-bodied reflection involving his whole being.

This sort of remembering, painful though it is, is the only way forward to honest forgiveness. It's a grueling process, calling us to reenter the valley of the shadow of death, to talk with a spiritual companion who will help us trudge through the fog of forgetfulness and the dark of denial, to walk again and again through the most painful and challenging moments of life, to weep and grieve.

Forgiving is not so much about forgetting as it is about remembering.

INCARNATIONAL REMEMBERING

It's possible to get stuck remembering, to obsess about painful events until they calcify into bitterness and cynicism or depression. The problem is not that we remember too much or too long, but that we remember too narrowly. The stories of forgiveness in our lives may seem like stories with two main characters—the perpetrator and the victim—but as long as we tell the story this way we will either have difficulty forgiving or we will reduce forgiveness to a therapeutic task whereby we forgive someone else in order to feel better ourselves.

If we understand all of life through the incarnation, then we see three people in every story of forgiveness. Jesus, who stands up for justice and against oppression, cries out on behalf of the powerless and is outraged at tragedies of sin in our world. Once Jesus made a whip and chased the sacrilegious money changers out of the holy temple; what sort of fury would he express toward those two youths who murdered and desecrated Ev's mother? What would Jesus say today about grown-ups who neglect children, about racial discrimination or political structures that give a few wealth while propelling others into poverty, or about charlatans who rob cancer patients of their money by preying on their fears? I imagine Jesus crying out in indignation, then weeping in great sadness.

This same Jesus who is filled with truth and justice is also filled with grace and mercy. Jesus came to live among us, to dwell with us in our brokenness, and to reveal God's great kindness to those who languish in this broken world.

I don't know why Ray chose a church parking lot for his remembering instead of Taco Bell or Wal-Mart or Sears, but I'd guess that he was inviting God into his remembering. In the depth of anguish, and in the midst of messy catharsis, Ray heard God's voice breaking decades of paternal silence. In that church parking lot he began to reflect on God's redeeming presence in his life, to see how tenderly God had cared for him as he had walked among his life's broken shards. Ray later wrote, "I got it. God was caring for me in the way a Father cares for a son!" In the midst of his turmoil and shame, Ray caught a glimpse of home and all the good things that are there.

Remembering is painful because it requires us to face our fear and shame. But pain opens us up if we stop and listen to it. We can keep running faster and faster to try to get away from pain—and sometimes that seems the easier way—or we can rest assured in the incarnation, knowing that God understands every throb of a broken heart. Having faith that God is with us can give us courage to stop, remember, and turn toward deep sources of meaning and hope.

Ray, who had been so deeply wounded by his father's alcoholism and apathy, continued to find help in counseling, and eventually became a professional counselor himself. As he immersed himself in Christian faith, Ray found the sort of fatherly love he had always longed for. He became actively involved in a church where he helps others explore and strengthen their family relationships. In all these ways he is moving from shame to hope. Ray puts it this way: "In dealing with my shame and grief I have found it necessary to face them many times over, to loosen their grip on me by identifying and supplanting the insidious messages that bind me. It is in this work of submitting myself openly and honestly before God and others that I am transformed most fully into a new creation, able to leave the past behind me and to lay hold of freedom."

I am moved by Ray's courage. How many of us would fold under lesser pressures, resigning ourselves to lives of bitterness or shallow achievement, or simply drown ourselves in the legacy of alcoholism? How many of us would keep moving in the trajectory established by the previous generation without stopping to reflect, without changing directions? Ray chose an incarnational form of remembering, inviting God to be with him in his pain, and ultimately found secure love in a spiritual home.

There is another part of incarnational remembering that I hesitate mentioning because it may seem to trivialize the suffering that many experience. It is sometimes shocking to remember that Jesus did not come to draw a line separating the good guys from the bad guys. Jesus came to save us from the sin and brokenness that permeate all of creation and every one of us. Both the good guy and the bad guy live inside each of us.

After living through the horrors of political incarceration under a communist regime, Aleksandr Solzhenitsyn—a Nobel Prize–winning Russian author—wrote about the human capacity for good and evil in *The Gulag Archipelago: 1918–1956:* "When I lay there on rotting prison straw . . . it was disclosed to me that the line separating good and evil passes not through states, nor between classes, nor between political parties either—but right through every human heart—and through all human hearts. This line shifts. Inside us, it oscillates with the years. And even within hearts overwhelmed by evil, one small bridgehead of good is retained. And even in the best of all hearts, there remains . . . an un-uprooted small corner of evil."[5]

If we craft a story with two neatly defined characters—the forgiver and the perpetrator—we have failed to see Solzhenitsyn's point and the point Jesus made many centuries before, that good and bad are commingled inside each of us. The wounded are also wounders, and wounders are also wounded. Who knows what sort of pain Ray's father faced earlier in his life with his own alcoholic father? The two youths who killed Ev's mother had no excuse for their crime, but what sort of life traumas shaped them into the murderers they became? What sort of potential for evil lurks inside each of us?

Remembering in light of the incarnation calls us to humility and even to empathy for those whose actions have hurt us. I have never committed murder and cannot even imagine doing so, but I am saddened and shocked by the wrongs I have proven myself capable of committing. My great consolation is knowing that God understands the struggles and temptations of life in a broken world, because Jesus came and lived among us. God understands, forgives, and loves us. Our capacity to forgive one another is merely a ripple emanating from God, who remembers us first.

Sometimes it sounds attractive to bundle up all the difficult things of the past in a large satchel, light a bonfire, and incinerate it all. Put it all in the past and forget it ever happened. But as appealing as doing this may seem, this repress-and-deny strategy is not the way we function best. Our greatest health—physically, spiritually, relationally, and emotionally—comes from unpacking the satchel and choosing to remember, inviting God to be with us in our pain, honestly looking at our own shortcomings as we consider how others have failed us, and ultimately releasing the pain by forgiving those who have wounded us. This process of forgiving and remembering may take a long time, but it leads to shalom.

SURPRISED BY BLESSINGS

Forgiving and remembering often bring unanticipated blessings. We may begin the journey of forgiveness for less than noble reasons—perhaps out of a sense of religious obligation, or so that we can be relieved of our burdens of resentment and bitterness toward another person. But in the midst of the forgiveness journey, or at least by the end of the journey, many people are surprised by the blessing it brings.

Blessed by Gratitude

One blessing is gratitude. Henri Nouwen described our tendency to split the past into two categories—the joyful and the painful. We sometimes try to remember the one and forget the other, as if the ultimate quality of life depends on the number of tally marks recorded on the positive side of the ledger. Though this may seem good at first glance, it ultimately robs us of the essentials that can be found only through pain and

struggle: our need for one another, opportunities to see goodness in others because of our weakness, our inability to control the circumstances of life, a capacity to learn from the past
as we move toward the future, and above all an awareness of
God's constant grace. A grateful life is not a life half-repressed,
but rather a life in which God is found everywhere. Nouwen
concludes that "true gratitude embraces all of life: the good
and the bad, the joyful and the painful, the holy and the not-
so-holy. We do this because we become aware of God's life,
God's presence in the middle of all that happens."[6]

It seems difficult to imagine that one could experience
gratitude in the wake of a gruesome murder, but after months
of working to forgive his mother's killers, Everett Worthington
did. In his book he writes, "Reflection on painful life events
has revealed the stain of unforgiveness in my own heart. As I
turned to God, God washed my heart—which had lusted earlier after the blood of the murderer—in the blood Jesus shed
at his crucifixion. I was forgiven; I could forgive. . . . I also try
to practice gratitude. I am grateful for what people can teach
me. I can also be grateful to God."[7] These words demonstrate
what spiritual writers have been emphasizing throughout the
centuries: that the virtuous life, the life of gratitude, is a life
disciplined with good remembering. By *good* remembering I
mean that we recall the bad things that have happened but
do not stop there. We go on to remember the ways we have
hurt others, and we still do not stop. Then we remember how
each of us has longed for mercy and forgiveness throughout
our days, and how utterly lost we would be without God's
grace. And we revel in gratitude that God is with us.

Blessed by Reconciliation

Another blessing that sometimes emerges from forgiveness is the joy of reconciliation. But the word *reconciliation* is both too big and too small. It is too big because forgiveness does not always lead to reconciliation. Sometimes reconciliation is simply not possible. Everett Worthington and others who study forgiveness are careful to distinguish forgiveness from reconciliation. Forgiveness is choosing to release feelings of hatred and bitterness and, perhaps, to develop feelings of understanding and empathy toward the offender. Reconciliation is to enter a restored relationship with the offender. Forgiveness is always advisable; reconciliation is not. For example, most would agree that the person repeatedly abused by a partner should leave the relationship rather than continue to reconcile after each episode. Forgiving the abusive partner is a good goal, worth the time and effort it will require. Reconciliation might be foolish.

But the goal of reconciliation can also be too small because it implies restoring a relationship to where it was before the offense occurred. Sometimes relationships become better than ever after forgiveness occurs. In my work as a therapist I have seen examples of relationships becoming stronger in the aftermath of terrible offenses.

Perhaps one partner has a sexual affair, betraying the other's trust and shattering their sacred vows of marriage. For a time the couple heads off into a wilderness of misunderstanding and bitterness. As time passes, they begin turning back toward each other, retracing their steps and finding their way back home to one another. Ultimately, the violated spouse forgives the wayward spouse. But there is more.

In returning home to one another, some couples can reclaim some beautiful and spontaneous part of love that they had not experienced before the crisis. They learn to see one another differently, to face problems they didn't know existed, and to reclaim something they didn't realize they had lost. In the aftermath of great pain they discover a love more beautiful than they had ever imagined. Parker Palmer, a renowned teacher and spiritual guide, writes, "Winter clears the landscape, however brutally, giving us a chance to see ourselves and each other more clearly, to see the very ground of our being."[8]

Of course not every story has a happy ending. Some people try to forgive but are never able to overcome the bitterness. Some spouses leave and never return. Some who long to be married never are. Children wander and struggle, and some never come home again. One person betrays another and never returns to apologize. Relationships can be excruciating, and some losses can never be restored.

But even here, in the midst of shattered relationships where we feel life's deepest pain, some people experience God's blessings as poignant, astonishing, and ultimately inexplicable.

Blessed Inexplicably

God's blessings cannot always be explained. Some are too big for human understanding, and our only proper response is to revel in God's goodness and to rest in the secure love of a God who is with us.

In 1993 Ray's father was diagnosed with cancer. Ray was well aware of his lifelong wish for his father to soften, to repent, to speak a blessing, and so he began seeking out his father. At first there was only one place Ray could spend time with his father, so he went to the bar where his father had wasted the best years of life. Week after week Ray sat sipping soft drinks in a smoke-filled bar on the south side of Chicago, listening to jukebox music and watching his father poison his liver with more alcohol. He offered small talk because there was nothing else to offer this man he had never known. He waited for a blessing, for a word of encouragement. Each week he waited.

Ray's father's health slipped until, in 1996, he could no longer leave his apartment. During the last two months of his father's life, Ray devoted a day each week to sitting by his father's side, caring for him and meeting whatever needs he expressed. Ray never received the soft words of remorse and blessing that he hoped for—his father was silent to the end— but with time he discovered the beauty of an inner peace he had never imagined. Somehow, somewhere, in the midst of administering pain medications, cooking meals, helping his father to the bathroom, and cleaning him up when he could not get there in time, Ray found blessings. Ray recounts, "In my heart I knew I was at peace with him. I no longer resented him. I had forgiven him and understood him. In fact, I loved him and felt compassion for him. In giving to him so willingly and with love, I had realized that I had overcome my need for him to give to me. . . . Those memories are God's blessings that affirm me, reminding me of who I am by the grace of a loving and healing God."

In this story, we again see the miracle of the incarnation. God came to us, to live in our messy world and walk among us. Divinity and humanity touched. Jesus became human—fully God and fully human—which means that hope, divine hope, now infuses our world and lives beside us and within us. God is with us, not just as a baby in a manger two thousand years ago, but in the darkest nights of loneliness and sadness, in the biggest social problems of our time, in the aftermath of abuse and exploitation, and in all the suffering that engulfs our planet. God is present in our schools and hospitals, in our places of worship, in symphonies and operas, in ballparks and amusement parks, and even in the darkened taverns populated by lonely, silent men. God, who grants humanity the free will to make the messes we live in, will never abandon us. Touched by God's mercy, Ray could not abandon his father. So Ray went to the bar, and he cared for his father in the final weeks of life.

The blessings God grants in the midst of life's rubble are more beautiful than we could have imagined. In our forgiving and remembering there is often something much bigger, something mysterious and even life giving, that emerges along the way. A flower blooms in the desert. A rainbow arcs across the sky. A refreshing breeze drifts across the landscape. Somehow beauty and goodness are reclaimed, and even the painful and regrettable events of the past are softened by the compassion of the present moment.

Ray's story is about a man overcoming his rugged childhood to forgive his father and become a caring and loving father of his own two sons, but it is much more than this. It is a story of faith; a story of coming home. Ray first learned to rest in the secure love God offers; then he could walk alongside his father. God took a man who had every right to nurse his anger for a lifetime and reclaimed his heart so thoroughly that he could serve a remorseless father, even as his father passed from life to death. I could employ various psychological explanations for such a thing, ranging from repression to self-actualization, but the simplest explanation—and, in my opinion, the best—is that our world reverberates with the wonder of the incarnation.

PART THREE

Looking Around

7

Home to Self

One of the things I often do is give speeches. I like doing it and enjoy being with people and sharing whatever insights I've gleaned from my research. One day, after I had just delivered a talk in Cincinnati about psychology, theology, and spirituality in Christian counseling, I was feeling pretty good. The talk had gone unusually well: the room was packed, people laughed in all the right places, our eye contact suggested that I had kept the audience's attention, and there was a good deal of head nodding to affirm me along the way. Afterwards, I was encircled with folks who wanted to talk. I noticed one young woman who seemed to be waiting until after everyone else had left. She succeeded, and soon it was just the two of us talking as we stood in the front of a large lecture hall.

As she began to speak I realized how young she must be—I guessed her to be not much older than my oldest daughter. She identified herself as a graduate student before giving a few words of congratulations on a good talk. I thanked her, though I had already been satiated with approval and was ready to pack up my equipment and go to a nearby Starbucks with Lisa.

"But I really disagreed with one point you made," she went on. This caught my attention because people rarely say such a thing directly to a speaker. Normally it is done in the hallway or the restroom with the hope that the speaker is not within hearing distance. It's always a gift when someone is bold enough to speak with me directly about points of disagreement. So I appreciated her candor as I listened to her concern, assuming it would be a simple matter of correcting her youthful misunderstanding.

At one point in the talk I had distinguished between Christian spirituality and other, more amorphous forms of spirituality that seem to be swirling around today. Spirituality ought to free us to experience God in personal and intimate ways, I said, but I sometimes wonder if we have become too free. It seems that spirituality can mean almost anything these days—from taking off one's clothes in a New Mexico hot spring to having a dream about a dead ancestor. I made the point that Christian spirituality has boundaries around it, defined by Scripture and historic Christian theology. So far, so good. But in the process of making this point I said something like this: "Contemporary spiritualities seem to be about finding ourselves, but a Christian spirituality is more about denying ourselves and finding God."

This woman told me she disagreed, saying that we need not deny ourselves in order to find God. She insisted that our best chance of finding God comes when we discover who God made us to be and celebrate our uniqueness. I explained that the notion of denying ourselves comes directly from

Scripture, from the words of Jesus in Matthew 16:24, and that many who speak of "finding" themselves for the sake of their spirituality are prone to narcissistic wanderings that lead them far from the Christian faith. She countered with descriptions of rigid Christians who fail to discover themselves and as a result seem to have no idea how poorly they relate to others, of those who think going to church on Sunday and believing certain doctrines are all that matters in life. I didn't deny she was right but spoke of those who abandon the faith because they think their personal insights, informed by several months of self-reflection, are more valid than the time-honored tenets of Christian theology, informed by many centuries of collective wisdom, debate, and scholarship. She argued her point for a while, then I argued mine, then she hers—verbal Ping-Pong in Cincinnati.

Then I used a phrase that every psychologist learns early in his or her career: "You may be right." What this phrase really means is, "I don't think you are right, but you and I will probably not agree no matter how long we discuss it, so let's move on. Starbucks awaits." I thanked her for her thoughts and told her I would continue reading and thinking about this. I did.

DENYING AND DISCOVERING

I now realize that we were both partly right, each of us representing a side in a lifelong challenge that confronts every person seeking to follow Jesus. She was saying we need to discover ourselves, and I was saying we need to deny ourselves. I now see that both are true, but somehow our words that day got tangled up with our desire to be heard by the other. To disentangle ourselves we needed the language of the true self and the false self used by spiritual writers for many centuries. The true self is the full, complete person we were each created to be as we walk securely in God's love. The false self grasps to meet our needs in our own self-serving ways, attempting to find satisfaction and meaning apart from God. This language helps it all makes sense: we need to discover our true self, as my discussant in Cincinnati reminded me, and deny our false self, as I reminded her.

When Jesus taught his followers to deny themselves, I don't think he was suggesting they stop caring about themselves or give up trying to understand who they were, but that they give up their selfish ambition and deny their false selves. Jesus went on to pose a paradox: "If you try to keep your life for yourself, you will lose it. But if you give up your life for me, you will find true life" (Matthew 16:25). I wonder if Jesus is offering an invitation more than issuing an ultimatum. It's not so much that he is pounding the pulpit and telling us to "just say no" to our selfish desires, but that he is offering a better way that ultimately leads to greater peace and joy than any life plan we could devise on our own. The pathway to the abundant life Jesus came to bring calls us to give up trying to engineer our own happiness and to discover true life in God.

The woman in Cincinnati was making an important point: knowing God and discovering our true self point us in the same direction. The more we know God, the more we discover our truest self, and the more we discover our true self, the more fully we will know God. John Calvin, a theologian influential in the Protestant Reformation of the sixteenth century, made a similar point at the beginning of his *Institutes of the Christian Religion* by suggesting that the knowledge of self and knowledge of God are inseparable. More recently, David Benner has made a compelling case for self-knowledge in *The Gift of Being Yourself.* He writes, "Deep knowing of God and deep knowing of self always develop interactively. The result is the authentic transformation of the self that is at the core of Christian spirituality."[1]

Discovering our true self in God is a journey that we will never fully complete in this life, but when we get glimpses of our destination it is an amazing experience. Perhaps you have days when you live close to the center of God's love. You don't feel particularly concerned about winning anything or getting your way, but enjoy the goodness of life even while you grieve the injustices and tragedies of our broken world. You treasure the uniqueness of human personality, the joy of work and leisure, and the opportunity to share yourself with others. Food tastes especially good. You feel grateful to God for the gift of life. On these days you might ask someone, "How are you?" and really mean it. You want to know and be known. On these days, you glimpse the fullness of life and the goodness of your true self. This is not a self to be denied; this is a self to be discovered and nurtured.

On other days we seem more prone to our false self, grasping and clawing to get somewhere or accomplish something we deem to be essential, focusing on the goals we have yet to achieve or the possessions we do not yet own, and complaining because others are holding us back. We may dwell in self-pity or some other form of self-obsession, and live far from the center of God's love. When we ask, "How are you?" we are hoping for a one-word answer so we can stay on schedule. This is the self we want to deny.

Described in these terms, it seems obvious that we would choose the true self, day after day. But it is not so easy. The subtle deception of the false self is overpowering, giving us the illusion that we are free when we are not.

ILLUSIVE FREEDOM

We hear and see countless "be yourself" messages, plastered as advertisements in every nook and cranny of our world. Each day we are told in a hundred ways, "Do what you want in the name of freedom or individuality or mental health. After all, you're worth it." These hedonistic messages may sell beer or mascara or new cars quite well, and they may even convince us that we are free to choose our own destinies, but their net effect is to propel us further into our false selves. Sometimes freedom is only an illusion.

We think that taking matters into our own control and looking for ways to assure our own happiness are the way to freedom. This is what the Prodigal Son thought when he asked for his inheritance early. "Give me my money and let me go to where I can be free and satisfied." But this is backward. The abundant life is at home with the father, not in a faraway land with illusive (and elusive) freedom. Only after his long journey home, and in the secure embrace of love, could the Prodigal begin to discover his true self—unique and significant, and cherished by his father.

Our true self is in synch with our yearning for God. Psychiatrist Gerald May begins his book *Addiction and Grace* with this observation: "After twenty years of listening to the yearnings of people's hearts, I am convinced that all human beings have an inborn desire for God. Whether we are consciously religious or not, this desire is our deepest longing and our most precious treasure."[2] Being in touch with our deep longing for God is our source of hope and freedom, but, like the Prodigal, we get this backward. Sometimes our lives become so cluttered with other pursuits that we fail to see or pursue our true longings. May goes on: "The longing at the center of our hearts repeatedly disappears from our awareness, and its energy is usurped by forces that are not at all loving. Our desires are captured, and we give ourselves over to things that, in our deepest honesty, we really do not want."[3] We exchange freedom for captivity.

The poignancy of our backwardness struck me while visiting the Turpentine Creek Wildlife Refuge outside Eureka Springs, Arkansas.[4] The refuge takes in exotic large cats in danger of being euthanized. Many of these cats were raised as domestic pets until their size and predatory instincts made them dangerous. The refuge now has more than one hundred lions, tigers, cougars, and bobcats. Gradually, as funds allow, the refuge workers are building outdoor habitats for the animals, getting them out of small cages with concrete floors and putting them in large half-acre areas where they can run and play and nap in the great outdoors.

The lions Samson and Esmeralda had recently been moved to one of the new outdoor habitat areas. Both were raised in captivity (presumably by someone who thought it would be fun to have a pet lion without considering that they grow to be eight hundred pounds), so until the date of the big move they had spent their entire lives in concrete-floor pens. Imagine the freedom they gained, going from a small prison cell to a half-acre natural habitat replete with grass and trees.

The day of the move came, and the refuge workers were looking forward to seeing the lions thriving in their new outdoor habitat. They were saddened to see Samson and Esmeralda head straight for the feeding area inside the habitat, where they found a pen with concrete floors. The lions have stayed there in an unlocked pen, day and night, ever since. When attendants once hosed the lions with water to get them outside the pen, Samson and Esmeralda wandered around outside for a few minutes and then came right back to their pens. They are locked in, whether by familiarity or fear or both, not realizing there is a much richer and freer life waiting for them outside the cage doors.

Like Samson and Esmeralda, many of us have too small a view of freedom. We have been raised in a sort of captivity. We think we know about freedom—we see it every day on the television screen, in the novels we read, and in the thousands of marketing devices that compete for our attention. We learn that freedom is found in financial success, in having all the pleasures of life accessible at a moment's notice, in great physical beauty. Our false selves have a deep hunger for consuming and possessing: houses and cars, jobs and titles, computers and cell phones, liposuction and teeth whitening, friends and spouses, psychotherapy and religion. None of these are intrinsically bad, but we too easily become attached to them and think they are the way toward freedom. Jesus offers another way; he invites us to come outside our habits and assumptions, to revel in the freedom of the true life.

I fear that even the religious structures of our faith sometimes hold us in captivity. The God who desires to make us free is not always represented well in our churches. I think of Randy, a man who wore a lapel pin rewarding him for attending church each week for the past twenty years. Randy described his marriage to Sharon in unembarrassed terms— how he had insisted she read her Bible for thirty minutes each morning, how she was not allowed to work outside the home or talk on the telephone with other men, and how she was required to submit unquestioningly to his wishes in managing the household and in their sexual relationship. He justified all this on the basis of his church's teaching and his understanding of the Bible. Then Sharon left, and Randy felt desperate, lost, and utterly alone. Here was a man who had invested enormous energy in what he thought knowing God meant but who had spent very little time trying to understand his true self and his relationships with others. He was living in captivity, and forcing Sharon to live there too, until she could take no more.

Now twenty years later, I still recall the sadness of our last session together. After several months of meeting with Randy, I came to the conclusion that I could not help him. To this day I don't know if he lacked the emotional resources to look at himself or if I lacked the ability to help him do so, but I know it was not helpful for him to sit in my office week after week and repeat his "Sharon is a vile sinner" rhetoric. Ultimately I realized it was not ethical for me to continue taking his money and his time if I could not help him, so we stopped meeting. It was difficult for both of us. Randy had to give up his dream that I could help him get Sharon back, and I had to give up my dream that I could get Randy out of his concrete-floor pen to enjoy the freedom of the great outdoors. Randy would have loved his true self. He had a delightful sense of humor. He loved to read and exercise and garden. He yearned to know God. But Randy was held in captivity by his insecurities and fears, sitting in an unlocked pen wondering why Sharon didn't want to sit there with him. His faith held the power to set him free, but the rigid religious structures surrounding his faith, and an equally rigid personality style, locked him up in fear. Randy and I both felt great sadness as we shook hands good-bye. I still feel it now, and I wonder what the past two decades have brought for this man who cared so much about knowing God yet did it so poorly.

The label "false self" can be confusing because it seems to imply that we build our identity on something that is utterly wrong. Not so. One reason we are so vulnerable to constructing false selves is that they contain a seed of truth. Randy built a false self around his frantic clinging to Sharon, but beneath his desperation was something good and right: he wanted to hold on to her love. Others construct a false self around an obsession with beauty, but the pursuit of beauty is also a good thing. God created incredible beauty in our universe and created us to love beauty, to be drawn to it, and to find ways of creating it ourselves. My tendency is to build a false self around achievement, assuming that my worth is measured by my accomplishments. This is surely a false self, drawing me away from God, but it is still based on a seed of truth. God created work and blessed each of us with energy and rationality and deemed it good. Our false selves are not entirely wrong, which is why they so easily seduce us, yet they ultimately push us in the wrong direction—toward the captivity of self-obsession and away from finding our free and true self in God.

Our supposed freedom to choose and build our own destiny keeps us imprisoned in our delusions of control. Eventually the false self masks the true self, so falseness starts to feel like the only option. Benner writes, "Everything that is false about us arises from our belief that our deepest happiness will come from living life our way, not God's way. Although we may say we want to trust God and surrender to his will, deep down we doubt that God is really capable of securing our happiness."[5]

Only by stepping outside of our false self—usually because of pain—can we begin to see it is false. Denying the false self may seem to be limiting our choices, but actually it opens the possibility of discovering the true self in God where we can romp and tumble in the vastness of the habitat God has created for us. This is the essence of faith: believing God has a better way than we can devise on our own.

A SOUL CALLED IDA

On my last visit to the Art Institute of Chicago, I wandered through various rooms filled with the work of famous artists, giving the paintings a cursory glance, wishing I understood the nuances of art better. Then I happened upon Ivan Albright's oil painting *Into the World There Came a Soul Called*

Ida.[6] The painting compelled me to stand and study it and then to go home and read more about Albright and his painting.

Ida is an aging woman wearing revealing clothes and sitting on a wicker chair while looking in a cosmetic mirror she holds in her right hand. Her body is old and lumpy, showing the relentless effects of time. Each lump and wrinkle is exaggerated to highlight the dilemma Ida faces. She has a powder puff in her left hand as she embarks on her futile attempt to disguise her decaying body. Her face is sad and wistful as she glances hopelessly into the mirror and attempts to reclaim the vibrancy of youth with a veneer of cosmetics. On the dressing table beside her sits a vase with dead flowers.

The painting, crafted at the end of the Roaring Twenties, is compelling enough as a work of visual art, but Albright's title makes it all the more intriguing: *Into the World There Came a Soul Called Ida.* Why did Albright choose the word *soul,* especially in an era when almost no one used that word? Today's fascination with spirituality has brought the soul back into vogue. Today there are thousands of books with the word soul in the title, ranging from *Chicken Soup for the Soul* to *Chicken Poop for the Soul* and *Pot Stories for the Soul* (published by High Times). Today automobile manufacturers sell luxury cars by convincing us that their cars are good for our souls. But back in the 1920s the word soul had almost disappeared from the English lexicon. Why did Albright use a near-extinct word normally found only in old hymnals and revival meetings to describe an aging woman sitting at her dressing table?

Many of Albright's paintings explore what art experts call the *vanitas* theme, which portrays the tension between the attractive pleasures of life and its fleeting nature. All the pleasures of life are hampered by time. A once beautiful woman sits in front of a mirror, but her beauty has left her just as the flowers at her side have withered. Life and death converge. So Albright's decision to call Ida a soul is a fascinating way to highlight the tension between the immediate and the eternal. Although I don't know Albright's spiritual vantage point when he crafted this painting, it seems he understood something of the false and true self. Ida is staring at the fleeting remnants of her false self in the mirror she holds, longing to find some meaning and significance in her life. She yearns for a true self.

I imagine Jesus entering a painting such as this with tears welling in his eyes. I imagine him holding out his arms and saying, "Ida, Ida. I have created you as a beautiful soul, unique and special, completely loved, cherished more than you can ever know. Set the mirror down, Ida. Deny your false self. Set aside the selfish ambition and all the pressure to become beautiful. Come home and see that you are already loved. Discover your true self in me. Let yourself live."

GROWING TRUE

In the beginning, we learn in Genesis, God created true selves. They frolicked and worked and laughed and played in their glorious habitat. They walked and talked with God. But then these true selves were seduced into thinking they could find more joy by stepping outside God's plan and making a "free" choice. A great falseness settled in, contaminating all creation. Looking for freedom, these selves took on the bondage of living in a broken, distorted world where they battled shame, fear, pain, disease, and death.

Every life in God is a journey back toward the true self we were intended to be—securely loved and unafraid. We will never fully arrive in this life because the damage of sin is too great, yet we keep journeying. With each step on this journey toward our true self, we also take a step closer to God, and with each step toward God we move closer to our true self.

The journey toward our true self and toward God begins with a turn toward redemption, a single step to reverse the direction our life is heading. It is often pain that causes us to step outside of our false selves and see that we need a new perspective. It is the grace of God that enables us to change our course. God is always working to redeem us, to convert the pain of living into an opportunity to see ourselves and our need for God more clearly.

I think of JoAnn, a young woman who had learned far too much about pain in her thirty-three years. After a series of three physically and emotionally abusive relationships, she decided it was time to deal with her depression and understand herself better. In therapy she began to explore how desperately she had always needed approval. She had longed for approval from her parents, who both worked until 7:30 each evening and rarely saw her. She had longed for it at school, where she was ostracized for being overweight. Now as an adult, having shed her extra pounds, she had not been able to shed her neurotic need for approval. Each time a new man came along and showed her some attention, she was putty in his hands.

JoAnn had to look back and remember, to grieve the past and connect her past experiences with her present-day vulnerabilities, but she also needed to discover herself in the here and now. Who was she? How was she unique and gifted? How could the pain and growth in her life help connect her with others in healthy relationships? We spent many weeks discussing these questions. JoAnn began discovering herself as one who is creative and fun loving, hard working and industrious, vulnerable to peer pressure, more artistic than intellectual, wounded by past rejections, a social person who especially enjoys children, and someone who cares deeply for her parents and wants them to be happy. She began gaining confidence as she looked honestly at her personality.

Then something happened. JoAnn came for our thirteenth session with a huge grin on her face. Something was different. A neighbor, Marlene, had invited JoAnn to church for the hundredth time, and this time JoAnn decided to say yes. Though raised in a religious home, JoAnn had come to think of God as hard to please and angry with her, so she left her faith behind as she entered adulthood. In therapy she began to see that her views of God were part of the larger fabric of her life: she yearned for approval but believed she was never quite good enough to deserve it. So armed with the new awareness of herself that she was gaining in therapy, she decided to accept Marlene's invitation. At Marlene's church— a place that emphasized the love and grace of God—JoAnn had a profound spiritual awakening.

She almost stood up and danced in my office, she was so happy. The transformation in her life was remarkable. We met for the next few weeks to make sure the changes were real, and occasionally over the next several months for purposes of maintenance and follow-up. Each of those sessions was a celebration. JoAnn had a breakthrough in her life, in both her understanding of herself and her understanding of God. We could quibble about which came first—better psychological knowledge of herself or her spiritual awakening—but ultimately it doesn't matter. The point is that discovery of self and discovery of God were pointing in the same direction. The more she discovered her true self, the more open she became to God's work in her life; and the more she experienced God, the more she discovered about herself. JoAnn had spent much of her life chasing the approval that proved to be so elusive, and now she turned to find her way home to her true self in God.

Of course this was just the beginning of JoAnn's journey. She has undoubtedly faced challenges and struggles in the years since her spiritual awakening. It takes effort to stay on course in following Jesus.

Because every true self is unique, I cannot offer a list of the top ten ways we can grow deeper in our life with God. You and I are different by God's design, so we will relate to God differently too. But even if we cannot derive a precise list of *how* we grow true in God, we can agree that it involves getting to know God.

I love the subtitle of Richard Foster's book on prayer: *Finding the Heart's True Home.* The true self longs to know God, to have conversation, to reveal emotion and express doubt and offer praise, to listen, to know and be known by God. My best Christian friends—those I know well enough to talk about prayer—tell me that prayer is their greatest struggle in the spiritual life. I find the same in my own life. Rather than causing us to cower in defeat, this ought to bring us hope. It means that in our truest self we yearn to have more time with God, just as we might want to have more time with a lover, though the realities of life make it challenging and difficult. There is something in the longing itself that helps us grow true, because it reminds us that we are created not only for the daily tasks of life but also for a love relationship with God.

In a committed love relationship, I am not fully my own but I belong to another. And so as the first question and answer of the Heidelberg Catechism have reminded us over the past 450 years, we are not our own. We belong to God.

It is difficult to remember whose we are. Just as Adam and Eve were drawn away from their true selves with a lie about finding greater freedom, so we are surrounded by voices that tell us to leave the journey toward God in pursuit of some pleasure presumed to be better or more thrilling. Rembrandt's *Return of the Prodigal Son,* which I have referred to in this book and in another, helps me remember whose I am. A replica hangs in my home office where I see it every day and remember that I am the broken, needy one who belongs to a gracious and forgiving God. This is the true self, embraced in love, engulfed in forgiveness, forever safe in the arms of grace.

When my friends and I talk about our desire for a fuller prayer life, we sometimes forget that prayer need not be relegated to sitting or kneeling with our eyes closed for twenty minutes in the morning. We also can open our eyes and see

God everywhere in our lives. In his book *Space for God,* Don Postema recommends that we say to ourselves, over and over, "I belong to God." After a while it becomes a very good habit, saying it ten times a day, or a hundred times, or a thousand: "I belong to God." It is so easy to forget whose I am, but these words of belonging bring me back, over and over, to my true identity.

The reason you read a book such as this, and the reason I write it, is to keep remembering whose we are, to keep journeying toward true life in God. It seems clear that we need reminders, and we need fellow pilgrims who are walking this journey with us. It is not an easy journey. We slip and fall, we lose our way, and we are continually tempted by the false voices around us. Still, we belong to God, and God calls us onward toward abundant life.

THE TANGIBLE SELF

The abundant life is filled with all sorts of sensations and experiences—tastes and smells, prayer, dancing, solitude, sensual delight, abundance and deprivation, adventure, celebration, pleasure and pain. I make this point because speaking of abundant life and finding our identity in God might easily lend itself to a Gnostic understanding of the true self. The Gnostics attempted (in the first centuries of the Christian church) to split the world into the material and the spiritual and then to call the material bad and the spiritual good. Jesus was not a Gnostic—indeed, the incarnation makes Gnosticism laughable—but many who have come after him have insisted on interpreting his words through a Gnostic lens. Some of the New Testament letters written by the Apostle Paul were confronting Gnostics in the early church. The Council of Nicaea (in A.D. 325) confronted and defeated the Gnostics, who argued that Jesus could not be God because a perfect God could not take on the foulness of human substance. A century later, at the Council of Chalcedon (A.D. 451), church leaders denounced the Gnostic notion that Jesus was not fully human. More recently the Gnostic controversy has been resurrected by books such as Dan Brown's *Da Vinci Code* and others that have speculated about the Gnostic gospels that were excluded from the New Testament canon. Over and over throughout history we see the Gnostic heresy breaking in on a more orthodox understanding of the faith. Underlying Gnosticism is the more ubiquitous assumption of dualism, which dissects the human person into body and soul. Dualism suggests that the human soul is an immaterial essence, a container of consciousness that coexists with the body and keeps living when the body dies. Can you imagine how boring heaven would be if we were just a bunch of disembodied souls haunting the cosmos? I suppose it could be fun on Halloween, but what would we do with the rest of eternity? I am grateful that the Christian view of heaven includes matter: a new body and a new earth. I am fond of my five senses and glad to think I may never have to give them up.

This may seem like splitting hairs, or like academic mumbo-jumbo—the old mind-body problem dressed up in spiritual language—but it is an essential part of understanding our true self. The true self is a tangible self: an embodied, material soul living in a physical world that God created. And it always will be.

This means the true self is not limited to immaterial spiritual activities—prayer, spiritual intuition, mystical experiences, and so on (even though these activities engage the body). If we are embodied souls, it means the true self can splash around in a cool mountain lake or savor a chocolate milkshake or offer a homeless person shelter for the night. True selves wake each morning, get stuck in traffic jams, love backrubs, get mosquito bites, and struggle to make ends meet. Maybe they even go hitchhiking.

The true self lives in all the splendor of creation, and in a broken world the true self languishes with all the struggles of life, too. The true self is not a flawless self, at least not this side of heaven. So even if we are becoming aligned with God, finding our true self and shedding our false selves, we still struggle with envy and lust and fear and a desire to control others. But rather than turning to chase after illusive dreams, we admit our struggles to God and beg for the grace to live with awareness of God's abiding love.

A colleague tells the story of a ninety-year-old stalwart of the Christian faith who came to Wheaton College as a chapel speaker many years ago. During a question-and-answer session, a twenty-year-old college male asked the speaker how many years a man typically struggles with lust. The speaker replied, "I don't know. You'll have to ask someone older than me." This chapel speaker was widely renowned as a person of great spiritual maturity, and rightly so. This was a true self speaking—one who knew his vulnerabilities, acknowledged his struggles, and still chose to follow God.

Coming home to our true self does not mean we arrive at perfection or escape life's troubles. It means we keep trying—by God's grace—to deny our false selves and to discover our true identity in the secure embrace of God, who loves us more than we can fathom and longs to show us the ways of abundant life.

8

Home to Relationships

Of all the blessings in life, good friendship is among the very best. Being with a good friend is like enjoying cool, fresh water after a long summer hike, quenching the thirst of the human soul. Clark was that sort of friend. There was a time when we would get together each week for lunch and then linger in the restaurant or walk along the streets of Newberg, Oregon, to talk about our families, our work, and our personal struggles and joys. I knew this was an important friendship when Clark dared to tell me I was putting my marriage at risk by getting too close to a woman friend. I hated hearing it, but he earned my trust with his bravery, and I soon came to see the wisdom of his counsel. Not all our talks were so intense. I remember bountiful laughter—loud, free, even bawdy mirth refreshing two lives that were sometimes quite parched by heavy workloads and the normal challenges of trying to be responsible husbands and fathers.

Every couple years I come across the picture our wives took in front of a Hooters restaurant. Clark and I are each products of a particular evangelical Christian subculture that makes going to Hooters a taboo of sorts. Besides, we are both sympathetic enough to contemporary feminism that we would feel vicariously offended for womankind as we pretended not to notice the scantily clad busty women servers. But one night Clark and I and our spouses were walking by a Hooters on the San Antonio River Walk when Lisa or Donell (Clark's wife) had the idea of taking a picture of the two of us standing beneath the Hooters sign. As we posed, two young women employees in traditional Hooters attire bounced out of the restaurant, pressed into us from either side, and said "cheese" right alongside us. There we stand, memorialized on film, with an awkward combination of junior high hormones, middle-aged geekiness, and evangelical guilt all merged into two of the goofiest grins in the history of the world.

Clark and I are still friends, but now twenty-three hundred miles separate us, as do the twelve years since we lived in the same town. Each year and each mile brings distance. We get together about once a year and go to lunch in Newberg, a baseball game in Toronto, a basketball game in Dallas, or a movie with lots of explosions in Chicago. The explosions make us feel manly, which seems more important than it used to. Every time we see each other I am reminded of how bittersweet life can be. There is joy in seeing one another again, sadness that it happens so rarely, and even greater sorrow that our closeness is slipping like sand through our fingers with each passing year.

It occurs to me that all close relationships are bittersweet. They meet our profound desire for connection, but every relationship eventually slips away through death or distance. We find great joy in the companionship of another, yet there is sorrow and loss in joy's wake. And it's not just losing a relationship that is difficult; many times the relationship itself is challenging. Some relationships are complicated—like the friendship that Clark warned me about—blending all the goodness of friendship with uninvited complexities. Other relationships are fiery and intense, balancing elation on the edge of disaster. It seems that some relationships are invested with potential but never bloom into the beauty both people hope for. A few relationships are long and steady, solid and sturdy, yet still the benign annoyances must be managed before they become a malignant mass of resentment and frustration.

Every current relationship, like every one from the past, is an alloy of grace and brokenness, of true self and false self, of victory and struggle. The challenge of living well in the present involves finding shalom in the midst of these imperfect relationships. The most fortunate among us are able to craft joyful homes even though marriages are flawed and children unpredictable, to forge deep friendships with other fallen human beings (the only kind, it turns out), and to come together in caring human communities despite the realities of hypocrisy, miscommunication, power struggles, and apathy. And beneath each of these present desires for home is our instinctual spiritual yearning: we crave the safety of God's love. It surrounds us every moment if we will just look around.

If you are like me, you yearn to find God in the messiness of human relationships. We look around, trying to find our way. We feel misunderstood. We are alienated from others.

We get lost and wander from those we love, and they wander too. Sometimes we even turn away and head off to live in the land of false selves. But God is always working whether we recognize it or not, always active in human affairs, always redeeming that which has been shattered, always loving those who deem themselves too far gone to love, always inviting people back together toward peace and reconciliation, always reminding us that we cannot out-sin God's grace, and always calling us to care tenderly for one another, as true selves do, with love.

THE FORCES OF SHALOM

Finding shalom in the midst of relationships involves living in the rhythm of coming home to the other person, time after time. Every close relationship is affected by two opposing forces (to use terms I've drawn from physics): centrifugal forces that hurl two bodies away from one another and centripetal forces that draw them back together.

Centrifugal Forces

The pushing away occurs for various reasons, some quite healthy. We push away from one another in order to keep a personal identity, an appropriate autonomy from the other. This need for autonomy can easily be overemphasized, and often is in Western individualism, but some degree of separateness is necessary for two people to be in a healthy relationship. People need to cultivate the capacity to stand firmly on their own, even as they still choose to stand together. In his famous poem *The Prophet,* Khalil Gibran writes, "And stand together yet not too near together: for the pillars of the temple stand apart, and the oak trees and cypress grow not in each other's shadow."[1]

We also end up at a distance because of factors beyond our control. Friends relocate, children move on, lovers are pressed into working long hours or living at a distance. Not long ago I was sitting on an airplane next to an army sergeant on his way home from a twelve-month tour in Iraq. He was effusive with the joy of coming home, but in his eyes I discerned a trace of uncertainty about what it would be like to see his girlfriend again, to be face-to-face after a year of communicating only by email and occasional phone calls.

Sometimes relationships are strained simply because staying close to another person is difficult. We say things imperfectly and hear the imperfect words of others through defensive ears, so we often end up feeling distant from those we want to be closest to. It is easy to think of the "big" examples—sexual affairs, domestic abuse, financial betrayal—but there are also dozens of little stressors in most close relationships. Probably every person in a long-term romantic relationship has a list of hassles; it may include chore distribution, toilet seat etiquette, table manners, parenting styles, heating and cooling preferences, and so on.

The better I know Lisa, the more I learn about her desire to conserve everything. She prints her work on scratch paper, avoids air conditioning, recycles, rides a fuel-efficient scooter to work, takes her own bags to the grocery store, and even takes flatware to fast-food restaurants in order to avoid using the plastic utensils they offer. And when doing her stint on long highway driving trips, she conserves fuel by using the brakes only in life-threatening emergencies. This has always been tough on her anxiety-prone husband, but it has become even worse now that our newest car—a 1999 Toyota—has cruise control. It's quite an experience, really. Sometimes I'll be sitting in the passenger seat noticing that the trucks in front of us are filling both lanes at sixty-two miles per hour. Lisa has the cruise control set at sixty-three. Slowing down is not an option. This means that within the next few moments someone will have to move, or we will be crashing into their rear bumper, just below the yellow decal that says "Tell me how I'm driving." I begin estimating the distance until impact: 500 feet, 200, 100, 50, 20, 10. This is when I close my eyes and imagine what eternity might look like.

It's amazing to see how it works out. A sympathetic driver moves out of the way at the last possible moment, or a quick lane-swerving maneuver on Lisa's part keeps us out of emergency flights to the nearest hospital. She's not had an accident yet, but next time we shop for a car I may suggest that we avoid cruise control.

There are, of course, two sides to this story. I had no idea what a nervous, micromanaging passenger I could be until we bought a car with cruise control. I am surprised by how grumpy and entitled I can act about where we set the thermostat in the summer. And, I'm sure, Lisa could tell stories about my annoying quirks (and probably will now, in her next book).

Obviously, describing conflicts about cruise control and air conditioning does not do justice to the depth of suffering that occurs in some relationships. These are trivial examples when compared to the deep wounding that sometimes happens in close relationships. Betrayal, contempt, abuse, addiction, bitter accusations, and past emotional scars contaminate close relationships and cause deep rifts between people. These strong centrifugal forces can sometimes be overcome with forgiveness and reconciliation, and sometimes they cannot. The reason I offer these seemingly trivial examples, such as hassling over highway driving methods, is because we often overlook their importance in daily life.

Think of having one little hassle in a long-term relationship as carrying one pebble along the journey of life. In itself, it's no big deal. Pebbles are light and easy to manage. If some other hassle comes up, then you have two pebbles. Still, it's not a big problem. But if these little hassles go unmanaged, and the pebbles keep accumulating, eventually they become weighty and drag you down. Caustic words slip out in a moment of annoyance, irritating habits drive a wedge between two people, a small misunderstanding festers in silence, one person insists on too much autonomy or too much intimacy. If we don't watch out for the small stressors in life, before we know it we are engulfed in anger and bitterness. And as much as we may want to blame the other person, both people almost always share the blame for a problem.

We collect pebbles not just because of the annoying habits others have but also because of our limited capacity to understand and love one another. Centuries of theological reflection and decades of social psychology research point to the same conclusion: we think more highly of ourselves than we ought. We overestimate our opinions. We blame others for bad things that happen to us while holding them accountable for the bad things that happen to them. We selectively seek information to buttress our beliefs while disregarding contradictory data, and often cling to false beliefs even when faced with irrefutable evidence to the contrary. All of this behavior can be labeled with one term: pride, one of the seven deadly sins—and rightfully so. It is deadly to us spiritually, physically, emotionally, and relationally. Pride keeps us from seeing the truth that we have failed to love our neighbors as ourselves.

Centripetal Forces

If we had only centrifugal forces pushing us apart in relationships, then eventually all of us would be alone and isolated or darting in and out of a series of short-term friendships. But the greater force propels us the other way, toward human relationships. Psychologists speak of human attachment. It seems to be instinctual, from the very first moments of life outside the womb, for us to relate with one another, to form connections. And these forces persist throughout most of our lives. We have an inborn yearning, intrinsic centripetal forces that compel us to mend broken relationships.

Praise be to God who created in us the centripetal forces to bring us back to one another. Think of the times you have returned, by God's grace, to relationships of secure love. Think of the pebbles you have dropped along the path as you have discussed and resolved differences with those you love. God delights in restoring broken, prideful people like you and me, because this is the God of the incarnation—the one who remembers us first, understands the confusion of the human heart, knows how challenging relationships can be, and longs for us to come home to places of secure love.

After a dispute with a friend or an argument with a partner, we typically feel an inner gnawing, a subtle discontent that tells us things are not right. We can ignore these feelings, and after years of practice some people may learn to disregard them altogether, but it is much better to listen. These are centripetal forces pulling us back together to affirm our care for one another. Jesus taught about this in his Sermon on the Mount, instructing his followers to give the highest priority to getting things right in their relationships, even if doing so means postponing worship. "So if you are standing before the altar in the Temple, offering a sacrifice to God, and you suddenly remember that someone has something against you, leave your sacrifice there beside the altar. Go and be reconciled to that person. Then come and offer your sacrifice to God" (Matthew 5:23–24).

Jesus is telling us to listen to the gnawing in our hearts, to turn back toward the ones from whom we feel estranged. We can get tangled up in exceptions, questioning if Jesus would have a person go back to an unrepentant and abusive spouse, but in doing so we miss the point. Although reconciling is not wise in every case, Jesus—the greatest reconciler of all—calls us to mend broken relationships whenever possible.

Most of us are moved by stories of renewal, of a marriage or friendship restored or a family relationship salvaged after years of silence. These are big examples that ought to be noticed, but if we look carefully we can see more subtle examples that might easily be missed in the scurry of life. I believe God would want us to notice.

I was at a professional meeting recently when a psychologist made a derogatory and unfair public comment about

Christians. I spoke up to register my concerns. The following day this same person caught me in the hallway to apologize for her comment. It was a gracious and sincere apology, and I was moved by her humility. I asked for more of her story, so she went on to describe some of the cruelty that she, as a lesbian, had experienced from Christians and how she ultimately decided to leave the faith. As she told me her story I was immersed in both sadness and gratitude—sadness that she had endured such malice from those wanting to follow Jesus, and gratitude that she would think to apologize for her comparatively trivial offense against me. Although she had left her faith behind and chosen a lifestyle that I find regrettable, I recognized the stamp of God's image on her soul. Her apology and my empathy for her situation were centripetal forces drawing us toward mutual understanding and the possibility of new friendship.

Life calls us—over and over again—to acknowledge our common humanity as well as our failure and the failure of others, to stand up after we are knocked over by shame or guilt or sadness or anger, and to return to the hope of authentic relationship. We fall down, you and I. Courage is not found in denying our faults or minimizing how others disappoint us, but in getting up again and again to build shalom in the midst of complex relationships.

DEEP WOUNDS, DEEP HEALING

There used to be an idealist lurking in me that said any relationship could be restored if both parties could learn to speak the truth and listen to the other. This idealistic part of me drove me to graduate school to become a healer, and went mostly unbridled through the early years of my clinical practice. Over the years my idealism has been suffocated by the cumulative experiences of life. For one thing, I find that people are not always willing to speak or listen to one another. Sometimes the wounding is too deep. And even when people want to come back together—to speak and listen and rebuild some lost part of their relationship—sometimes it is too late to undo the damage that has crippled both of them.

The death of my idealism, which was based on overconfidence in psychological healing, has helped me see how truly remarkable it is—both psychologically and spiritually—when lives are healed. Some relationships are healed after the deepest sort of wounding occurs, and when the healing happens I stand in awe of the magnificence of God's creation. Another person might gaze into the sky on a clear night and wonder at the dazzling beauty and sheer volume of God's handiwork, or look into a microscope to see the intricacies of cellular harmony—each part working together to sustain and even reproduce life. That's what I experience when I witness the splendor of two people's coming back together into a close and caring relationship. To me, this reveals some miraculous part of the way God works in our midst. God delights in our coming home *to* relationships.

But there is a still deeper mystery, a deeper healing. God also delights in drawing us home *through* relationships. Some relationships hold the power to heal unresolved wounds from the past. This, of course, is the premise of psychotherapy, but it also reveals the enormous potential of healthy friendship and romance and parenting and spirituality.

Andrea is a young woman with a remarkable story of deep wounding and healing. She has a scar on her knee that is much more poignant than the physical damage caused when her biological father put out a cigarette on her leg. Raised by abusive biological parents for the first three years of her life, Andrea was then removed from the home and became a ward of the state. She spent the next nine years in foster homes and a group home, curling up with books, talking with animals in the barn, and making up stories about princesses and mermaids. Andrea now recalls, "During the summers I would crawl into the huge lilac bush down near the bay with one of the cats and sit there with a book, breathing in the fragrant aroma, listening to the silence, and then watching the sun set into the far-off ocean." Andrea knew about sunsets and far-off things. She had no friends at school, and the friends she made at the group home soon disappeared just as surely as the sun slipped below the horizon each night. Andrea recalls waiting futilely for the mail carrier to bring a letter from her mother or father, and perking up each time the telephone rang for the first several years of her placements. Then, at the tender age of eight years, she gave up on ever hearing from them again.

Four years later, when Andrea was twelve, her parents suddenly reappeared and whisked her away to a small yellow house with a bright green door. The dreams Andrea had stopped daring to dream had come true, but only for a week. All hopes for her new existence were soon shattered by her father's relapse into drunken rages and the unspeakable abuse of incest. Six months later she was back in the group home, forever separated from the only family she knew.

Meanwhile, an ordinary family in another part of the country sat in a suburban church learning about adoption. After several months of contemplation and preparation, this family of five stood at Midway Airport waiting for Andrea to make them a family of six. Andrea remembers the moment vividly—walking off the plane in her blue jeans and Los Angeles Lakers T-shirt, having her new mother hand her a Care Bear and then bend down to give Andrea the first hug she recalls ever receiving. And the wound in Andrea's soul, like the one she once had on her knee, began its slow journey toward healing.

Although most of us have easier lives than Andrea, each of us has been wounded by others, and sometimes the circumstances of a broken world do not allow the wounds to be healed before one person dies or moves away or shuts out conversation. And so we limp onward with unresolved wounds, often sealing off the difficult things in the past because they are unpleasant to think or talk about. But then, if we are fortunate, we come across another human being who cares enough and is safe enough that we can gradually open the sealed memories of the past and reveal them. And the mystery of healing takes over. I wish I could explain this healing, but even after twenty years of doing psychotherapy I do not fully understand it. It remains mostly mysterious to me, but I have learned to trust its simple rhythm and to give praise to God that we are wonderfully and fearfully made.

Those with the courage to traverse the grief and the fear of looking back, and with the wisdom to bring the wounds of the past into present conversation, typically find healing and hope at the end of the journey.

Andrea's healing journey did not end at Midway Airport—it began there. It was difficult for her to adjust to the Midwest and connect with her new parents and siblings, and nightmares chased her from across the country. In her recurrent dream, Andrea would be running through her house trying to find a place to hide from her abusive biological father. She would run into a room, curl up in a corner, and cover her head with her trembling hands. She woke up in a cold sweat just as her father was reaching down toward her. Somehow Andrea's new mother could sense when these nightmares were happening, and she knew enough not to burst into Andrea's bedroom, which would have frightened Andrea even more. So her mother would knock lightly, then stand at the door for fifteen or twenty minutes whispering to Andrea that she was safe and that no one was going to hurt her.

Healing is a slow process. Andrea now recalls her aloofness, how she stayed detached from her adoptive family and did not know how to respond to the kindness they offered. She behaved more perfectly than any teenager can .be expected to behave, partly because of fear. She now recalls, "I was deathly afraid I would get sent back to my biological parents, but somehow I could not articulate that fear. I was afraid to do anything that might even mildly upset my adoptive parents because I thought they wouldn't love me anymore, or worse, that they would." Andrea couldn't dare to trust her new family's love because she didn't want to invest herself in something that might be taken away later. Wisely, her family seemed to know to give Andrea space without pushing too hard for her healing. Andrea honed her vocabulary skills by doing crossword puzzles with her mother. She sat in comfortable silence with her father, because they both enjoy silence. When she left the house for a few hours her father would call out, "Get in trouble." Andrea would smile because those playful words relieved some of the pressure she placed on herself. Her parents came to her sporting events, and at some point Andrea realized she liked having them there. She started to feel loved. But love is a disruptive thing. When the security of love began seeping into Andrea's life, she began recalling more about her childhood abuse and glimpsing the magnitude of pain and trauma in her early years. She struggled silently, afraid to share her inner turmoil with anyone.

With time, Andrea dared to open up to her older sister, Melissa, who was grown and out of the house. A beautiful friendship developed. Melissa held Andrea's hand through the gynecological exam that confirmed that her past sexual abuse would prevent her from having children. Then, to soothe the pain, they went to Melissa's apartment, shed some tears, ate ice cream, and watched movies until Andrea fell asleep on the couch. On another occasion, after Melissa learned that Andrea had bypassed the childhood joy of fairy tales, they curled up on the same couch and Melissa read children's stories to Andrea, whisking her away to never–never land where cows jump over the moon and people live happily ever after.

Andrea was attending university when the attacks of September 11, 2001, happened. One very early morning, at 3 A.M., Andrea found herself on the floor of the dormitory shower. The terrorist attacks had aroused some memories from her childhood that kept her from sleeping. As she sat in the shower, weeping and crying out to God for help, she looked again at the scar on her knee. Slowly, through her tears, she began seeing it as evidence of God's healing touch. She now reflects, "that wound produced out of anger and violence had since been healed by love and tenderness into a perfect pink scar. My scars are evidence of a painful past, but also tangible evidence of a healing God. I lay on the shower floor a bit longer, letting the warm water and the love of God run over me, comforting me in my brokenness. In the middle of the night, midst my grief and nakedness, I found God my Comforter, God my Redeemer, God my Father."

Andrea's story is not about the power of psychotherapy. Her healing occurred through everyday relationships in a normal family with their quirks and imperfections. This is the sort of miracle that is built into the fabric of creation. Healthy relationships heal us. They help us find our way home to places of secure love, where people sit in comfortable silence and someone whispers just outside the door that everything is going to be okay and cows jump over the moon.

Andrea carries a scar, reminding her that she is not completely cured and never will be this side of heaven. She has no early childhood scrapbooks, and if she did they would hold bad memories. Sometimes she awakes at 3 A.M. with awful memories and vivid nightmares, and perhaps these will recur throughout her life. She will not give birth. But her scar also signifies healing—a deep healing that comes only to those who have the courage and good fortune to face their suffering.

Henri Nouwen put it so beautifully: "it is precisely here, in that pain or poverty or awkwardness, that the Dancer invites us to rise up and take the first steps. For in our suffering, not apart from it, Jesus enters our sadness, takes us by the hand, pulls us gently up to stand, and invites us to dance."[2]

PART FOUR

Looking Up

9

Home to Jesus

Like so many, I was raised in a religious home—praying before meals, attending Sunday services, seeking to follow God's will for my life. I remember getting two Christmas presents in ninth grade—a new pair of skis and a new Bible. Honestly, I was more thrilled with the Bible than with the skis (though both gifts made me ecstatic about my generous parents for a few days). I remember wondering in those youthful years why anyone would choose a life apart from Jesus. As I grew toward adulthood I began to understand their reasons. The faith I had loved as a child began to feel cumbersome, restrictive, and onerous. Still, I held on even as I noticed many of my church friends slipping away, leaving the faith behind as they negotiated the new challenges of love, work, and personal identity. I wondered where their lives were leading as I oscillated between envy for their freedom and sadness for their waywardness.

It seems strange now that I never did leave. Maybe I watched others closely enough to realize that their freedom didn't always bring happiness. Or maybe that Bible I started reading in ninth grade seeped deep enough into my psyche that faith became my native way of seeing the world. Perhaps I didn't leave my faith because I didn't need to; my parents were wise enough to give me plenty of freedom as an adolescent, so I had no need to rebel against their authority and their faith. Or maybe I did leave my faith (and still do today), but would come back quickly enough that I hardly recognized the leaving.

It was easy for people to leave faith and family values in the 1960s and 1970s. The sexual revolution, Vietnam, and Watergate stirred things up. Cynicism had its day, and people left all sorts of values behind as they searched for a better way. Young people traded in the Eucharist for love-ins and peace marches, and had some important things to say in the process. But now that the incense has burned and peace marches are over and the spray-painted Volkswagen buses are sitting in wrecking yards, it seems that many in my generation (and other generations too) are looking back and wondering if they may have left something important behind.

In my work, I have seen people struggle with leaving and coming home to faith many times, and I am aware that some who read this book will be in the process of finding their way back. It is not easy. There is fault to be found in institutionalized religion—because religion, like all other endeavors, is plagued with human frailty. Some look at hypocrisy in the church and conclude they should avoid religion altogether. Also, we are overwhelmed with information and choice today, so to some it seems ignorant and offensive to return to particular truth claims which teach that one way is better than another. Many have been wounded by the arrogance and insensitivity of religious zealots and so are hesitant to identify with organized religion. Others have come to value freedom as a cardinal virtue, so any religion that claims a right to restrict freedom is viewed with suspicion. But still, despite all these obstacles, many people experience a deep inner hunger that calls them back to faith.

FINDING SPIRITUALITY

It seems that an increasing number of people are interested in embarking on a spiritual quest to find a higher power these days. This interest in spirituality is encouraging, reflecting a growing awareness that something or someone is bigger than any individual person. Each of us consists of several billion cells constructed of carbon-based atoms. These cells repair and reproduce themselves for several decades until they can do so no longer, and then we die. If that is the whole story—dust to dust—then we have good cause for hopelessness, but today's renewed interest in spirituality indicates that we know in our hearts that there is more to the story. We are not alone. We do not exist in the darkness of isolation.

One recent morning I rose early to pray, adopting the time-honored posture of kneeling. I closed my eyes and folded my hands—just like the old Sunday school pictures of how people pray. As I began talking with God I noticed an unusual darkness in my visual field. Of course I should expect darkness with my eyes closed, but this had an unusual intensity to it, and the darkness seemed to be growing by the second. It was more than what I would expect just from closing my eyes; this was like being abandoned by the light, as though I were becoming blind. This grew for several minutes until I felt myself surrounded by utter nothingness, alone in the universe. This is not what we expect or hope for in times of prayer. We want God to speak, to be close by, to shine divine light into our lives. But this particular morning the darkness was a gift, helping me see what life might look like if I truly were alone in the cosmos. In the abyss of darkness I considered the first line of a well-known prayer of St. Francis of Assisi: "O Most High, glorious God, enlighten the darkness of my heart." As I prayed, the darkness gradually waned to the beautiful reassurance that God is with me, loves me, and cares to hear my thoughts and feelings. My experience in prayer reminded me that I am not alone, while giving me a glimpse of the terror of isolation.

I don't pretend to know if such an experience can be explained by physiological processes. Perhaps my blood pressure was a bit lower than normal on this particular day, or something unusual was happening in the occipital cortex. Or maybe my choice to kneel affected blood flow to my brain. Perhaps. But I hope I never become so satisfied with naturalistic explanations that I close myself to the possibility of some greater presence in my daily experiences.

The spiritual quest reminds us that we are not alone. We begin looking outside our own assemblage of carbon-based atoms to explain things. Thus the alcoholic admits to being powerless and yields control to a higher power. The overachieving businessperson learns to meditate or pray, in recognition that the meaning of life is bigger than the bottom line. A cancer patient encounters an inexplicable inner peace that aids in healing. New parents begin going to church, realizing that they want to nurture their children's spirituality.

As much as I am encouraged by renewed interest in spirituality, there is something about the vagueness of the generic spiritual quest that makes me feel uneasy. Theologians probe the historical tension between the transcendence and immanence of God, noting that Christian spirituality affirms both. God is high above us, transcendent in all ways, yet is also with us, immanent in our day-to-day world. If we lean too far in the direction of transcendence without considering immanence, we risk deism—the belief that God is a remote Creator not particularly concerned about or involved in the daily operations of the universe. But if we teeter the other way, toward immanence without transcendence, we venture into pantheism, which asserts that the divine is everything and everything is divine. In pantheism, there is no room for the person of God to exist outside of creation. My uneasiness with today's free-form spirituality is that we may be leaning toward pantheism.

The vagueness of today's spirituality can be illustrated by looking at the items on popular spirituality inventories. We psychologists develop pencil-and-paper instruments to measure just about everything. We measure body image, personality, marital satisfaction, self-esteem, attachment style, and hundreds of other things. (A colleague and I even developed a way to measure skill at the popular table game Trivial Pursuit and then had our fifteen minutes of infamy when the local ten o'clock news decided to do a "look how psychologists waste their time" special feature.) Not surprisingly, psychologists have also attempted to measure spirituality. If you were to take one of the leading spirituality inventories you would be asked if you believe there is one true faith, and if you were to say yes you would be deemed less spiritual than if you answered no. The scholars who developed this instrument assume that the purest spirituality is open and inclusive, with no particular faith commitments. Inclusiveness has great merit, especially when one considers the oppression and discrimination that have occurred in the name of religion over the centuries (and Christians have done their share of the oppressing). But still, there is something disquieting about a spirituality that avoids particular faith commitments. In our inclusiveness we may have forgotten to articulate the nature and object of our spiritual search.

As good as it is to find our way back to renewed spirituality, I believe there is more to be discovered on the path toward home.

FINDING GOD

From a Christian vantage point, there is risk in trying to find spirituality within ourselves or in the world around us without giving homage to a transcendent being. The Christian faith asserts that God is Creator and we are the creatures God created; God transcends us, existed before us, and is supreme over all creation.

If God transcends us and is the author and standard of truth, then this takes off some pressure. It means we are not left to figure out truth on our own. When people say, "listen to your heart," I think they mean it to be encouraging, but I find it quite frightening. I believe there is great darkness in my heart and that my greatest hope is finding a truth that exists outside of me. Like that first line from St. Francis's prayer, "enlighten the darkness of my heart," I need God to be transcendent and much bigger than me if I am to discover truth.

And it's not just that my heart is dark. I am also quite sure that my particular time and culture keep me from understanding certain aspects of God's character. A couple of centuries ago, God-fearing men and women went to church and worshiped each Sunday and then returned to their plantations, where they held human lives in bondage. How could they have been so blinded by their time and culture? And in what ways am I equally blinded today?

If God is transcendent and God's truth bigger than any particular epoch or culture, it means we get the clearest view of God by looking across history to find the truth that has been distilled by faithful saints throughout the centuries and has stood the test of time. It calls us to read books—old books—and to learn from those who have studied the past. We are called back to Scripture, to Athanasius and Augustine, to the Councils of Nicaea and Chalcedon, back to days when thoughtful scholarship was considered more important than spiritual experiences, back to a time when doctrinal disagreement was not presumed to disqualify the possibility of transcendent truth. In the process we discover that morality is not simply a matter of personal conscience or democratic process, that heresy must certainly be named and even rebuked. This sort of theological remembering beckons us to return to deep cisterns of wisdom.

It seems to me that we need to look up high to find God, much higher than looking to our own hearts. This majestic

God, the author of truth, is worthy of all praise and honor and glory forever. But if we look for God only in lofty realms of transcendence, we easily neglect that God is also immanent. God is here with us, bursting with love for humanity and eager to extend grace.

Many folks—even some identifying themselves as Christian—seem content to worship God without paying much attention to Jesus. In this they look too high, because if we really want to know God we must learn to see Jesus, the one who walked in our midst. Jesus, God incarnate, is the crystal-clear revelation of God's nature. The author of the New Testament book Hebrews writes, "The Son reflects God's own glory, and everything about him represents God exactly" (Hebrews 1:3).

FINDING JESUS

The idea of finding our way home to Jesus may evoke images of a fire-and-brimstone evangelist slowing the pace of his rhetoric as he pans his arm across his body and drawls out the word "JEEEE-sus." There are better images. Think of the time Jesus got angry with his followers because they were trying to keep children from bothering him. Jesus gathered the children to him, affirming their faith. He touched them, and blessed them. This is the Jesus I want to find.

I am drawn to the Jesus who looked at people who couldn't walk or see or hear, and reached out in compassion to heal them. He cared for whole people—body and soul. And if I am truthful, I must also add that I am attracted to

Jesus because he did much of his healing on the Sabbath, thereby calling religious leaders back to the compassion and mercy that inspired the rules they tried so diligently to follow. Jesus put meaning back into religious ritual while demonstrating that he is Lord of the Sabbath and Lord of all, full of truth and grace.

I want to know the Jesus who spoke out against oppression, who calmed the lives of men and women just as surely as he calmed the raging sea, but stirred folks up too when they needed to be challenged. This Jesus gave up his work as a carpenter so he could hang out in fishing villages on the shores of Lake Galilee and talk about God's good news, though it must have seemed like very bad news to those who hated and eventually killed him. Still, he kept on speaking the truth.

This same Jesus had a good friend, Peter, who denied even knowing Jesus in order to save his own skin. Jesus was led away to die for Peter's sins, and yours and mine too, while Peter ran off and wept bitterly for his failure. Sometime later, after the miracle we celebrate each Easter, Jesus found Peter back at the lake early one morning and cooked him breakfast. I need to sit with this Jesus, because I too am prone to deny him and run off and then to weep for my failure. I want to spend early mornings with Jesus, to let him find me like he found Peter, to hear his gracious voice, and to express my love for him.

Theologians split how we look at Jesus into two categories. A view from above begins with the theological conclusions we have about Jesus, hammered out by church councils within the first few centuries after his death. A view from below begins with the historical accounts of Jesus' life on earth, trying to view Jesus apart from the later theologies describing his nature and work. Both are attractive. I want to know Jesus from below, to see him as he was and not just as he showed up on flannel boards during my childhood Sunday school lessons. The Jesus we know from Scripture hung out with sinners and shocked people with his anger at injustice. He raised his voice against the proud and even called them names; he confronted revered religious leaders and chased entrepreneurs out of the temple with a whip. Jesus grieved for the people of Jerusalem and spoke of how he longed for them to come home. He experienced more physical pain than any person should have to endure, and he also suffered intense emotional pain—even to the point of sweating drops of blood. He was gracious to those in need, a true friend to many, a healer, an incredible teacher, a man of prayer and grace and compassion. He cared for his mother even as he was dying. I love viewing Jesus from below, but I need more than a role model. The Jesus I want to find must also be viewed from above because something magnificent happened three days after he died on a cross. It was so startling that his closest followers radically changed their lives: they didn't go back to their fishing boats to grieve the loss of a good friend, but went on to establish the apostolic church that formed the practices and doctrines shaping Christianity over these many centuries, and ultimately they gave their lives as martyrs. The Jesus who changed these apostles' lives holds power over death itself, and the influence of his transcendent saving work is still resounding today as it will through all ages.

Jesus suffered in the garden as he anticipated his death; then soldiers arrived and hauled him off to be questioned by unscrupulous politicians, accused by angry mobs, and ridiculed by soldiers, who also flogged him with a lead-tipped whip. Jesus stooped and staggered before his accusers without calling down legions of angels to smite them all dead. Then Jesus, the Christ, was stripped of his clothes, pierced with nails, and taunted with insults, mockery, and a crown of thorns. Even then, in the toughest hours of life and death, he offered grace to a criminal hanging beside him and asked his heavenly father to forgive those who took his life. Then he died. I am drawn to this Christ who saves, taking on the sins of the world even as he demonstrated the limitless love of God and displayed victory over all the forces of evil. This Jesus—the "visible image of the invisible God"—is filled with grace and compassion, and is worth searching for even if it were to take our whole lives to find him (Colossians 1:15). Or maybe it's more a matter of sitting still long enough to allow Jesus to find us.

The God revealed in Jesus is a God of amazing grace. This is not the sort of grace that can be fully captured in a hymnal, a theology text, or even in the pages of Scripture. This is grace incarnate, grace that lived and died among us, grace that truly is greater than all our sin. If we want to understand this grace, we look at Jesus. Randall Balmer is a religious scholar and author who has spent a good deal of his adult life trying to rebuild a meaningful faith in the aftermath of his fundamentalist childhood home and church. Balmer's search led him to Jesus. In his book *Growing Pains: Learning to Love My Father's Faith,* he writes,

I began to catch a glimpse of this Jesus. I was sitting in church just before Christmas when suddenly the sermon faded to black, I turned my head upward, and in some intuitive way that I cannot explain, I saw Jesus. Not the Sunday school Jesus I thought I knew and found I didn't like very much, but a Jesus of compassion, the man of sorrows acquainted with grief. This is the Jesus who wandered in the wilderness for forty days and forty nights. This is the Jesus who was betrayed by his friends. This is the Jesus who embodied the abandonment of all humanity, who while hanging on the cross, suspended between heaven and earth with his arms outstretched, cried out in despair and sadness and utter abandonment . . . , "My God, My God! Why have you forsaken me?"[1]

It seems important that Balmer glimpsed Jesus while sitting in church. Sometimes we think of church as the place for people who have everything figured out, or at least think they do, but Balmer went to church because he doesn't have things figured out. If I am honest, I have to say I am a lot like Balmer in this. There are many things I don't have figured out, but most Sundays I have the sense to know where to go to receive help along this journey. Over and over, I go to church to find the grace of Jesus.

It is no coincidence that we call today's church the "body of Christ," because the life of Jesus is at the center of the Christian church. We have all sorts of churches these days—Orthodox and Catholic and Protestant of various stripes. The common denominator of every Christian church is that Jesus is at the center. Churches are messy places, of course, because they are led by men and women with messy lives who minister to messy people living in a messy world. But the church is still a beacon of light, as it has been since the time of Jesus, striving to bring truth and grace into a broken world. Churches throughout the world are feeding the hungry, clothing the naked, engaging in political activism, comforting the weary, sheltering the homeless, speaking out against discrimination and oppression, proclaiming the good news to lost souls, inviting people to come in from the cold to the warmth of God's love. Recent research demonstrates that churchgoers enjoy various sorts of physical and emotional health benefits when compared to non-churchgoers. I heard one leading health researcher say it bluntly: "Get your butt in church." I'm not so motivated by the health benefits, but if coming home to Jesus means going to Jesus' house, then church is exactly where I am heading.

Sometimes we look too high up or too far away for God. The good news—the gospel—of the Christian faith is that God is not so high up or far away after all. God is with us, revealed in Jesus, inviting us to come as we are, clothed in the messiness of humanity.

10

Home to Heaven

The Internet was never intended to be a study of human nature, but it is difficult to imagine a better one. It may be as close as we will ever get to an international tabula rasa, a huge blank slate where contemporary individuals and institutions can inscribe their very nature. Some call it a superhighway, but maybe it should be called a super-Rorschach. Admittedly, some cannot afford computer access or have little interest in new technologies, but the rest of us are leaving our virtual fingerprints all over cyberspace. The Internet allows everyone with a computer and an online connection to visit and create websites, revealing who they are and what they care about. This same technology allows us to count how many people visit various sites, how much money they spend there, and even how many milliseconds they linger. What we find in this grand study of human nature is both heartening and dismaying. The Internet reveals that we are people who love ideas, poetry, music, classic literature, humor, medical knowledge, religion, innovation, art, education, and pictures of grandchildren. But it also demonstrates how we are prone to exploitation of others for profit, to exhibitionism and voyeurism, and to appalling vulgarity.

After reviewing several books about heaven in preparation for this chapter (five of them purchased online, revealing something of my human nature), I decided to go to the Internet—this contemporary repository that reflects human nature—to see what I could learn. I typed "heaven" into Google, a commonly used search engine, and discovered that heaven is perceived as the place where we can get what we want. I found Programmers Heaven, with 26,836 files, links, and articles to explore, replete with source code and JavaScript. I found myself wondering if this is the site where the makers of plastic pocket protectors advertise, but all I could find were banner ads for global positioning systems (GPSs). Then I found Screen Saver Heaven, with a huge selection of ways to protect your computer screen and be entertained at the same time: movie action figures, models in swimsuits, a wide-eyed kitten, cartoon characters, sharks swimming in a tank, and exploding fireworks. There were no GPS ads to be found. Then there was Nerd's Heaven, filled with more computer stuff, and Rugby Heaven, with everything you want to know about the latest injuries. The backdrop for 8-Track Heaven looked like a tie-dyed T-shirt, and a place called Dog Nose Heaven began with the question that keeps us all awake at night: "How many times have you wasted hours on end, scouring the Web, searching for that perfect picture of a dog's cold, wet nose? Admit it, we all have. Take heart, *proboscis canis* admirers. Now, you can find all the dog noses you could dream of, all conveniently located in one place!"

The common theme in all these sites is that heaven is where we find what we want, and lots of it: dog noses, programming code, 8-track tapes, or whatever else your heart longs for. At first I shook my head in disagreement, thinking that heaven isn't about us. It's not a place where we get what we want. Then I paused, thought again, went back to all the books about heaven scattered around me, and ultimately nodded in agreement. This is exactly what heaven is: it is where we find what we want, what we have always wanted.

We have always wanted to be home, surrounded in the security of perfect love and understanding. Sometimes we obscure this great good, this deep longing of our heart, by filling our lives with lesser good things or with distractions, and yet the longing persists. It may burst out in a telephone booth along a highway, as it did for me in 1993, or in moments of quiet reflection in the middle of the night, during frantic moments when the demands and troubles of life seem out of control, or while sitting at a loved one's funeral. Being home, embraced in security and love, is what we want. It is what we have always wanted.

In heaven what we want and what we have will be perfectly aligned. Today, as we live in our broken world, the alignment is never quite right. It's like turning the focus ring on a camera, trying to bring the camera into perfect focus but never getting it exactly correct. But someday all will be in focus—our desires and our environment in perfect adjustment.

AS GOOD AS IT GETS?

In the acclaimed 1997 movie *As Good as It Gets,* Melvin Udall is an obsessive-compulsive romance novelist, played by Jack Nicholson, who walks into a psychiatrist's office and demands an unscheduled appointment. The psychiatrist refuses, sending Melvin back into the crowded waiting room where he pauses, looks around, and poses the question, "What if this is as good as it gets?" Someone in the waiting room gasps at Melvin's words, which is exactly the right response. This line haunts me. It rings in my ears, reminding me that it is one of the most important questions of life and death. What if the alignment between what we want and what we have is as focused as it will ever be? What if this life is as good as it gets?

If it is, then put this book down. You are wasting valuable time. If the security of home is limited to distant memories of childhood homes or to today's homes where we gather several times a week for meals and once a decade to eat watermelon and take photographs at extended family reunions, then our heart's desire for home is faint and disappointing. We may as well resort to cynicism or hedonism or work so hard that we never stop and think about the futility of it all. But if there is something inside you that tells you otherwise— some spring of hope suggesting there is more, then you are asking a bigger question.

So let's venture toward that bigger question: What if this *isn't* as good as it gets? This question is bigger because it dares us to hope and dream, to imagine a day when goodness prevails and all our desires are perfectly aligned with the circumstances of life.

Ultimately, we all have to decide by faith whether we are living in a one-act play or a three-act play. If it is a one-act play, then we are in the midst of a slow progression from life to death. Just as each individual life begins and ends, so it is with humanity. Something started us in motion a long time ago, now we live in the midst of an aging earth, and eventually the globe will warm too much or our resources will be depleted or we will destroy one another with our anger and our technology, and humanity will die as a result. We'd better look around and savor each moment because this is as good as it gets.

But if we are living in a three-act play—creation, fall, and redemption—then the progression is from full life to compromised life and back again to full life. The Christian story begins with utopia in the Garden, then abundant life is shattered by human rebellion. But God is at work, always redeeming that which is broken, and will ultimately offer perfect and complete redemption to those who will follow. Arthur Roberts, Quaker philosopher and author, puts it succinctly: "Death is not the last word. Life is the final word."[1]

We languish now, stuck between Eden and heaven, but still we see God's redemptive work all around, and this gives us hope for abundant life.

Don't get me wrong. There is much joy to be found in this life—in lingering conversations under starlit skies, in music and art and dance, in growing old with one you love or in hoping it will be so, in good food and drink, in quiet reflection and corporate worship, in established friendships and new ones, in parents and children and spouses. Sometimes I say "Life is good" tritely in response to some trivial thing that has gone my way. Perhaps I have found a parking spot near the store's entrance or remembered to pack my toothbrush on a business trip, and I say to myself, "Life is good." But life really *is* good. All around us we see love and hope and joy and peace. Our memories remind us how much we humans care for one another, how we long for connection, and how beautiful it is to hold one another close. Life in this world is good, and we are wise to savor the goodness, but if we are living in a three-act play then this is not nearly as good as it gets.

I doubt Melvin Udall intended to divide humanity into two categories when he asked that question in the psychiatrist's waiting room, but that is what he accomplished. The way we answer the question will determine the way we live our lives. Sixteen centuries ago, Augustine made a similar division of humanity in his classic work *The City of God*. Augustine described two cities. One, the earthly city, lives as if this world is as good as it gets. Self-interest trumps interest in God. The other, the heavenly city, recognizes the brokenness of today's world and lives as a community of sojourners in anticipation of God's final justice and mercy. An amazing future awaits.

If you dare to believe that this world *isn't* as good as it gets, then you are already in Augustine's heavenly city. You, like me, believe we are in the midst of a three-act play, alienated for a time, languishing in the gaps between what we want and what we have, but living with the hope of heaven.

To some these may seem like the escapist musings of a religious fanatic, and if this world is indeed as good as it gets, then these critics will be right. I will have wasted precious time writing this book, and you will have wasted time reading it. But if there really is an ultimate home called heaven, then this world is not as good as it gets, and one of the best things we can do is learn to hope for the life yet to come. C. S. Lewis put it starkly: "either there is 'pie in the sky' or there is not. If there is not, then Christianity is false, for this doctrine is woven into its whole fabric. If there is, then this truth, like any other, must be faced. . . . There have been times when I think we do not desire heaven but more often I find myself wondering whether, in our heart of hearts, we have ever desired anything else."[2]

ALIENATED AND ASKEW

It is difficult to align what we want and what we have because both are askew. At one level it sounds crazy to suggest we don't know what we want. We want what we want—a new stereo, a closer relationship with that person who works at the corner restaurant, a roof that doesn't leak, 10 percent more income. But in our fallen world, where we don't understand ourselves fully, our immediate wants sometimes veil the deeper longings of our hearts. The thrill of the new stereo goes away in a few hours or a few weeks, the new relationship turns out to be fraught with misunderstanding, new roofs cost too much, and a 10 percent raise leaves us wanting another 10 percent. These things we want are partly right, but they don't plumb the depths of our most profound human desires.

We do not fully know the longings of our heart because we live in a world of alienation. Even as I write these words I look out on the front lawn and see a robin's nest that has fallen from a tree. Yesterday Lisa saw the baby robins floundering in the grass alongside the nest. They have been removed from their home, alienated, knocked loose from the paradise of an old ash tree by a Midwest thunderstorm. They will probably survive, but they are disoriented, bruised, and confused. So are we.

The Christian narrative is a story about being knocked from the ash tree, but not forever. We were created for Eden, for a world without the brokenness of human rebellion, though we now live in a fallen existence where we only catch faint glimpses of paradise. Many times we do not even think to look up and remember where God intended us to live and where we will one day soar. But even when we forget to look up, there is still an inner tug telling us that this world is not quite right, that we are intended for something more. We sense our alienation, and this is what points us toward the hope of heaven and to the true longings of our heart.

To some it may seem dismal to emphasize our alienation, but to the Christian it is the basis of hope. Being alienated means that our instincts about this life are correct—things aren't quite right. It means we are searching for something more than a good marriage, a long life, a solid reputation, or a secure retirement. These are all good, but they do not meet the deepest desires of the human heart.

Sometimes we get glimpses of what we really want, and in these moments we soar in the ecstasy of everything good as we rise above the normal routines of life to see some higher truth, something noble or beautiful that might easily go unnoticed. When you're looking in the eyes of a child with a disability and you realize how much you want a world where everyone is treated with dignity, where everyone can learn from everyone else, then you are glimpsing something of what humans really want. When I stand on the Oregon coast—the place I most associate with the splendor of heaven—and am mesmerized by the rhythm and majesty of waves caressing the shore, then I am glimpsing some part of the beauty I have always yearned to know. These are moments when our sight is enlarged to view some bigger landscape of reality, when we see our homesickness for what it is. But even in these moments of clarity, when we feel the deep longings of our heart, we are left with a gap between what we want and what we have because the world around us is not right.

We want justice. When someone we love is killed by a drunk driver, when poverty means that a child goes hungry or without medical care, when discrimination translates into unequal opportunity and indiscriminate hate, our hearts cry out for something better. So we do what people made in God's image ought to do—we invoke our judicial system, form new organizations, and advocate for policies to curb the injustice. All these efforts are noble and right, and justice happens for some, but is this really as good as it gets? We still have oppression and war and economic imbalance around the globe. We want equal opportunity, but workplaces are still plagued with discrimination and abuses of power. Some people in affluent countries have the newest video games and backyard swimming pools and shiny new SUVs while others across the ocean are sold into sex slavery. Some of us have immense warehouses just down the street stocked with every sort of food imaginable, and our dilemma is whether to buy salmon or steak for dinner. Others languish in starvation and would gladly feast on our table scraps. Some of us have medical clinics with state-of-the-art facilities and health care plans that pay the bill, while others cannot afford to take a sick child for help. Things are not right. The haves and the have-nots live in different worlds, separated by a chasm of injustice. Now pause and imagine a place where justice rolls down like a mighty ocean, quashing all oppression and evil. Picture a place of opportunity and possibility, where human worth has nothing to do with net worth. Think of an existence without disease and hate, without litigation and special interest lobbying, where the expressions of our humanity are no longer smothered by the inhumane things we do to one another. Someday the justice we want and the justice we will have will be perfectly aligned.

We want freedom, but that is not what we have. We fight for it and write songs about it, and even rename our fried potatoes "freedom fries" if it seems politically expedient. Our yearning for freedom has inspired young men and women to give their lives in battles throughout many centuries and continents. One of them was a young, articulate African American man who gave his life in the civil rights battle of the 1960s. Martin Luther King Jr. had a dream for freedom, enunciated on the steps of the Lincoln Memorial in 1963 in his famous speech, "I Have a Dream." His dream was that someday African Americans—indeed, all Americans—would be "free at last." Forty years later, we have a day marked on the calendar in memory of Dr. King, and important steps toward civil rights have been taken, but many Americans have become jaded and cynical about the possibility of achieving this sort of freedom; the work is hard and slow, and fraught with hidden individual and institutional biases and misunderstandings. Of course we ought to keep working for human freedom, but we also ought to stop and imagine the possibility that this life *isn't* as good as it gets. Perhaps there really will be a day when we are free at last. And it won't be the me-first freedom of so many self-help gurus, but the freedom to choose rightly, to live in harmony and understanding with others, to celebrate diversity, to dance and sing in worship, to leap and frolic in the wonder of creation.

We cry out for inner peace, so we turn to stratoloungers, headphones, fishing, spiritual retreat centers, long walks, and warm baths. And we seek outer peace with others, too, from next-door neighbors to nations on the other side of the globe. As just about any beauty contestant will attest, we want world peace. But even with all our talk of peace, it seems difficult to find. Life rushes forward, and we are often left tumbling in the wake of chaos and misunderstanding. If we dare to hope, we remember that this isn't as good as it gets. We envision a day when peace means much more than the absence of conflict, when distinguishing between inner and outer peace will make no sense because everyone and every relationship will be immersed and saturated in shalom.

Most of all, we want love. Songs of love are carried on radio frequencies throughout the world. Desire for love drives people to pubs and dating services, to clothing stores and bookstores, to gyms and cosmetic surgeons. We are born to love and be loved. It is our destiny from the first moment of life, when our eyes open and we begin scanning the bright horizon, to find another set of eyes to fix our gaze upon. But what we want and what we have are poorly aligned, so love

relationships disappoint us, whether they are romantic, famil-
ial, or platonic. People leave. Love fades. Priorities change.
Selfishness prevails. Sometimes lovers become enemies and
innocent people get wounded in the crossfire. Sometimes sex
and love get all tangled up, causing people to think that the
pleasure of sexual climax is truly as good as it gets. But what
if it isn't? What if our understanding of love is pale and weak
compared to what we will one day know? Imagine the possibilities of heaven, where there is a love that surpasses the
thrill of new romance and exceeds a parent's love for a child.

In Chapter Eight I told the story of Andrea, a severely
abused girl who found a place of safety through the love of
her adoptive family. As she described the hope she finds in
God's faithful love, she told me there are days when she gets
so homesick for heaven that she can barely breathe. Some
might suggest this speaks of the depression and hopelessness
of a young woman who has been so badly damaged in this
life that she needs to invent myths about life to come in order
to feel hope, but I think otherwise. I think these are the words
of a woman who has learned to hope—one who has experienced enough pain to glimpse her heart's deep longing for
the security of home, and enough healing to believe such a
thing is possible. Andrea dares to look at what she really
wants, and when she does it takes her breath away. Perhaps
all of us are so homesick for heaven that we are just barely
breathing, all of us gasping and grasping for something so
beautiful yet still out of reach.

Peter Kreeft, a Christian philosopher and author,
describes alienation as our greatest blessing because it points
us to heaven. "Earthly dissatisfaction is the road to heavenly

satisfaction."[3] He goes on: "Alienation is the opposite of being at home. If the Bible is not wrong when it calls us 'strangers and pilgrims,' then that's why we feel alienation. We feel what *is*. . . . Heaven is *home*."[4]

OUR STORY, BY WATER

Someone recently gave me David James Duncan's nonfiction book, *My Story as Told by Water*. It is a book that is part biography, part political activism, and part spirituality; and, as the title implies, a river runs through it. Duncan is a masterful fiction writer—perhaps one of the best of our day. He has an amazing capacity to turn a phrase, to develop characters, and to spin a compelling story. When I read his novel *The Brothers K*, I kept wondering how anyone can learn to use words so well. But Duncan should probably stick with fiction. He is a better novelist than metaphysician. To his credit, he acknowledges his propensity for narcissism in *My Story as Told by Water*, and he demonstrates some humility in the subtitle, which could be a short chapter in itself: *Confessions, Druidic Rants, Reflections, Bird-Watchings, Fish-Stalkings, Visions, Songs and Prayers Refracting Light, from Living Rivers, in the Age of the Industrial Dark*. But still, I found this book disappointing. Duncan seems to think truth should be determined by the things that cause us wonder, rather than seeing wonder as being caused by the things that are true.

Despite my grumpiness with his theology, Duncan's images of water are lovely, inspiring me to reflect on heaven as our story as told by water. The story of heaven is *our story* rather than *my story*. This is an important distinction, because heaven does not lend itself to personal rants or spiritual meanderings. Hoping for heaven comes from the story of a *people* rather than the story of a *person,* a story told by people of Christian faith throughout many cultures and over many centuries. It is the story that gave hope to African American slaves toiling fourteen hours a day in the southern cotton fields, that comforted early Christians as they were rolled up in wax and burned as candles in Nero's stadium, that inspired hymn writers and artists to speculate on heaven's grandeur, that brought hope to Japanese martyrs in the seventeenth-century purging of Christianity, that has helped people of faith throughout all times defer gratification and dare to find hope in the darkest moments of life. It is *our* story because it reflects some near-universal yearning for something beyond earthly existence.

C. S. Lewis, the great twentieth-century Christian apologist, used our ubiquitous desire for heaven to argue for its existence. He argued that every innate human desire can be satisfied—food can sate our hunger, water can quench our thirst, friendship and romance can meet our desires for companionship and love, and so on. Lewis then goes on to demonstrate that through all time, humans have experienced an innate desire for something beyond this earth. We long for something more. Thus, because our inborn desires always correspond with some tangible means of satisfaction, it stands to reason that something beyond our earthly existence does, in fact, exist.

Our story of heaven is the time-honored account of a people rather than the spiritual speculations of a person. Heaven is hope, conceived in faith, for those who yearn to live and love and work and laugh and worship together in community, and who someday will.

Heaven is also a story told by water. Like water, heaven is tangible. Though it may slip through our fingers for a time, it is real enough to remove the grime and thirst of living. Water washes over us. It cleanses and refreshes. It quenches our thirst and sustains our lives. Sometimes we picture heaven as life in the clouds, as wandering souls drifting to-and-fro in the cosmos. But the Bible speaks of a new heaven and a new earth, of new bodies and new creation. Water will be part of the deal. I envision majestic waterfalls, serene lakes, and streams of living water. I love the imagery in C. S. Lewis's book *The Great Divorce,* in which heaven does not consist of ethereal landscape and bodiless creatures but of solid materiality. So solid, in fact, that the water can be walked upon, yet the currents of abundant life still flow. And like the rest of the physical world, it is sensuous, fully textured. Christianity, and the heaven it promises, affirms our senses. Kreeft writes, "Only Christianity truly glorifies the senses. Plato thinks they are the prison-house and obstacle to consciousness. Aristotle thinks they are only feeders, raw material for consciousness. Buddha thinks they are distractions and illusions. . . . All of them are wrong; all miss the glory."[5]

Heaven, like water, will fill our senses. It will be a place of desire and passion and adventure. Someone recently suggested to me that we will have no more desires in heaven. I think she meant to say that our passions will no longer run amuck in heaven, but if this is accomplished by removing all human desire then I shudder at the implications. It means we really will spend eternity as some of us learned in Sunday school, sitting emotionless in an eternal worship service, dressed in white robes, singing "Kumbaya"—all one million verses—over and over. I'm sure we will have incredible times of worship in heaven, but they will not be divorced from human desire. In fact, they will probably be all about our desires in relation to God's provision. We will dance and sing and revel and fall in humble reverence in the presence of God almighty, as our heart's deepest desires are simultaneously expressed and fulfilled. And there will be no need to contain our worship in church buildings. I suspect our worship will extend to all of life, because it will be abundant life. So swimming will be worship and so will mountain climbing and conversation and sitting beside a quiet stream. I'm hoping for basketball in heaven, too, and maybe I'll learn to high dive or bungee jump over water, and it will all be worship; all done in gratitude for the saving work of Jesus. Maybe on some starlit night you and I can sit on a dock somewhere on the shore of a shimmering lake and have a long conversation about how fulfilled we are and how we had no idea how deep and wide and high true life could be.

Jonathan Edwards, the great American theologian who, sadly enough, may be best known for his sermon "Sinners in the Hands of an Angry God," also delivered an amazing sermon about heaven in 1738. He titled it "Heaven Is a World of Love." Throughout his sermon, Edwards used metaphors of water to demonstrate the glory of heaven and the purity of love we will experience there. He refers to God as the fountain of love, just as the sun is the fountain of light. Think of it. The one who created love, from whom all love flows, will be our eternal home. "There in heaven this fountain of love, this eternal three in one, is set open without any obstacle to hinder access to it. There this glorious God is manifested and shines forth in full glory, in beams of love; there the fountain overflows in streams and rivers of love and delight, enough for all to drink at, and to swim in, yea, so as to overflow the world as it were with a deluge of love."[6]

This deluge of love will wash us in forgiveness. God knows, we need it. Perhaps we will be immersed deep into the Jordan River where all our sins will be washed away and our wounds healed. Today each of us could come up with a list of failures and reasons to flounder in guilt, but then the list will simply decompose in the river of life. We will emerge from the water of forgiveness into arms of eternal grace, where all our struggles and wanderings will be set aside, our souls will be cured, and we will be home at last.

LOST AND FOUND

Our quest for home is a story of secure love—about having it, losing it, and finding it again. In the three-act play of life, we're probably more in the losing it phase right now, but we can still find our way home. Or maybe it would be more accurate to say that home can find us, even when our impulses seem to take us away.

One afternoon when Lisa and I were coming home through O'Hare International Airport, we encountered a little seven-year-old girl we later found out was named Chloe. We watched as Chloe raced toward the tram leading from Terminal 1 to the remote parking lot at O'Hare International Airport.

She led the way as her mother wheeled a baby stroller and held a toddler by the hand. Chloe bounded onto the tram, ponytail bouncing and freckled face smiling, then turned to watch as the glass doors began to close between her and the rest of her family. She reached out her hand and cried out, "Mommy," but by then it was too late. As our tram went off to its next stop, Chloe's face and her mother's both crumpled into fear and anxiety.

I write this book because I empathize with Chloe. It seems to me that we are all lost in a way, or in a hundred ways. We are alienated and separated from places of secure love. It is so easy, so natural, to charge ahead in life without realizing what we might be leaving behind, and as a result we sometimes find ourselves quite lost in the daily matters of life. How often do we charge forward, heading toward the next promotion, seeking relief from pain, striving for material markers of success or the next thrill, without realizing that we are moving too fast or in the wrong direction, moving away from sources of secure love? It may be that we are distracted or seduced or deceived, or perhaps we are just much weaker and prone to sin than we think, but whatever the cause of our misdirection, the truth is that we sometimes get lost.

Lisa and I decided to get off with Chloe at the next tram stop, to wait with her until her mother arrived on the next tram. My hope is that this book is a bit like that—an opportunity for me to wait with you, and you with me, as we figure out what to do next. Perhaps you are in a strained relationship and longing to find your way home to a person you still care about. Maybe you have left behind important moral values and are trying to reclaim the person you once

187

were. Possibly the faith of your childhood is looking better with each passing year, and you are wondering how to recover it. For my part, I am a middle-aged man in a fairly privileged life who is prone to all these wanderings and more. I find I must come back, over and over, to the relationships and values and faith that define me and give me joy and purpose in life. I am both lost and found.

But there is also a bigger story I have tried to tell in this book. It is not just that we are lost in the various circumstances of daily living but that each of these circumstances serves as a living metaphor for a larger truth about being lost, wandering outside of Eden, until we are found by God. In this, Chloe represents all of humanity. We have charged ahead to follow our own paths and have ended up alienated, reaching out for God just as Chloe stretched out her hand and cried, "Mommy."

Fortunately, Chloe's mother was a fast thinker. She got on the emergency phone system and had the PA announcer tell Chloe to wait for her at the Terminal 2 tram stop. Chloe didn't need to spend time searching for her mother, because her mother was coming to find her. Eight minutes later, mother and daughter were reunited, and together they got back on the tram to head home. We could spend our whole lives searching for God, but God has a better plan. God, revealed in Jesus, came to meet us in our alienation and fear. And God still comes, in the darkest moments of life and in the brightest moments and the average moments, too, to comfort and care for us, to show us the way to abundant life, to lead us home to places of secure love. Someday that home will be unimaginably complete and beautiful.

When Chloe was racing toward the tram in Terminal 1, she was preoccupied with getting there as fast as she could. But a few seconds later, as the tram pulled away with her mother and siblings on the other side of the glass door, she understood what she really wanted. In the pain of her alienation she saw her longings for love. I imagine later that night, as Chloe nestled into her familiar bed, she smiled and thanked God for being home. She was home, where she was close to her mother, where she had everything that is truly important. What she wanted and what she had were aligned, and she rested secure in the presence of love.

Notes

Chapter One

1. David Benner, *Surrender to Love* (Downers Grove, Ill.: InterVarsity Press, 2003), p. 24.
2. Richard J. Foster, *Prayer: Finding the Heart's True Home* (San Francisco: HarperSanFrancisco, 1992), p. 1.
3. Mark Buchanan, *Unseen Things: Living in Light of Forever* (Sisters, Oreg.: Multnomah, 2002), pp. 41–42.
4. Frederick Buechner, *A Room Called Remember: Uncollected Pieces* (San Francisco: HarperSanFrancisco, 1984), pp. 21–22.

Chapter Two

1. Mark Buchanan, *Unseen Things: Living in Light of Forever* (Sisters, Oreg.: Multnomah, 2002), p. 75.
2. "The Man Poll," *Newsweek* (June 16, 2003), p. 53. The numbers cited do not add up to 100 percent because 10 percent reported not knowing how long they will live.
3. C. S. Lewis, *Mere Christianity* (Old Tappan, N.J.: Macmillan, 1952), p. 94.
4. Richard J. Foster, *Prayer: Finding the Heart's True Home* (San Francisco: HarperSanFrancisco, 1992), p. 9.

Chapter Three

1. Frederick Buechner, *Telling Secrets* (San Francisco: HarperSanFrancisco, 1991), p. 33.

2. Frederick Buechner, *The Longing for Home* (New York: HarperCollins, 1996), p. 128.
3. J. I. Packer, *Knowing God* (Downers Grove, Ill.: InterVarsity Press, 1973), p. 26.
4. C. S. Lewis, *The Great Divorce* (Old Tappan, N.J.: Macmillan, 1946), p. 44.
5. Frederick Buechner, *A Room Called Remember: Uncollected Pieces* (San Francisco: HarperSanFrancisco, 1984).
6. Frederick Buechner, *Telling Secrets,* p. 66.

Chapter Four

1. Leo Tolstoy, *The Death of Ivan Ilyich,* trans. Lynn Solotaroff (New York: Bantam Books, 1981), p. 120.
2. Ibid., p. 118.
3. Wallace Stegner, *Angle of Repose* (New York: Fawcett Crest, 1971), pp. 11–13.
4. Henri J. M. Nouwen, *Bread for the Journey: A Daybook of Wisdom and Faith* (San Francisco: HarperSanFrancisco, 1997), entry for January 6.

Chapter Five

1. Henri J. M. Nouwen, *Lifesigns: Intimacy, Fecundity, and Ecstasy in Christian Perspective* (New York: Image Books, 1990), p. 39.

Chapter Six

1. Everett L. Worthington, *Forgiving and Reconciling: Bridges to Wholeness and Hope* (Downers Grove, Ill.: InterVarsity Press, 2003).
2. Ibid., p. 21.
3. Henri J. M. Nouwen, *Turn My Mourning into Dancing* (Nashville, Tenn.: W Publishing Group, 2001), p. 16.
4. These words come from Ray's unpublished account of his relationship with his father. I describe the story with Ray's permission.
5. Aleksandr I. Solzhenitsyn, *The Gulag Archipelago: 1918–1956,* abridged by E. E. Ericson Jr. (New York: HarperCollins, 2003), p. 312. (Originally published 1973)

6. Nouwen, *Turn My Mourning into Dancing*, p. 17.
7. Worthington, *Forgiving and Reconciling*, p. 158.
8. Parker J. Palmer, *Let Your Life Speak: Listening for the Voice of Vocation* (San Francisco: Jossey-Bass, 2000), p. 102.

Chapter Seven

1. David Benner, *The Gift of Being Yourself* (Downers Grove, Ill.: InterVarsity Press, 2004), p. 30.
2. Gerald May, *Addiction and Grace: Love and Spirituality in the Healing of Addictions* (San Francisco: HarperSanFrancisco, 1988), p. 1.
3. Ibid., pp. 1–2.
4. More information is available at http://www.turpentinecreek.org.
5. Benner, *Gift of Being Yourself,* p. 75.
6. An electronic replica of the painting and more about Ivan Albright's work can be found online at the Chimera Gallery, http://www.cegur.com/Albright/Ida.html.

Chapter Eight

1. Khahil Gibran, *The Prophet* (New York: Knopf, 1923), p. 16.
2. Henri J. M. Nouwen, *Turn My Mourning into Dancing* (Nashville, Tenn.: W Publishing Group, 2001), p. 13.

Chapter Nine

1. Randall Balmer, *Growing Pains: Learning to Love My Father's Faith* (Grand Rapids, Mich.: Brazos Press, 2001), p. 22.

Chapter Ten

1. Arthur O. Roberts, *Exploring Heaven: What Great Christian Thinkers Tell Us About Our Afterlife with God* (San Francisco: HarperSanFrancisco, 2003), p. 33.
2. C. S. Lewis, *The Problem of Pain: How Human Suffering Raises Almost Intolerable Intellectual Problems* (Old Tappan, N.J.: Macmillan, 1962), pp. 144–145.
3. Peter Kreeft, *Heaven: The Heart's Deepest Longing* (San Francisco: Ignatius Press, 1989), p. 62.

4. Ibid., p. 66.

5. Peter Kreeft, *Everything You Ever Wanted to Know About Heaven but Never Dreamed of Asking* (San Francisco: Ignatius Press, 1990), p. 91.

6. Jonathan Edwards, "Heaven Is a World of Love," in Wilson H. Kimnach, Kenneth P. Minkema, and Douglas A. Sweeney (eds.), *The Sermons of Jonathan Edwards* (New Haven, Conn.: Yale University Press, 1999), p. 245.

The Author

Mark R. McMinn teaches at Wheaton College, where he is the Dr. Arthur P. Rech and Mrs. Jean May Rech Professor of Psychology and coordinator of the Center for Church-Psychology Collaboration. Mark holds a Ph.D. from Vanderbilt University. He is a licensed clinical psychologist, board certified by the American Board of Professional Psychology, and a Fellow of the American Psychological Association.

His previous books include *Why Sin Matters: The Surprising Relationship between Our Sin and God's Grace,* and *Psychology, Theology, and Spirituality in Christian Counseling.*

Mark and his wife, Lisa—a sociologist and author—live in Winfield, Illinois, and have three grown daughters. Mark enjoys playing basketball, doing home construction projects, and taking long walks with Lisa.